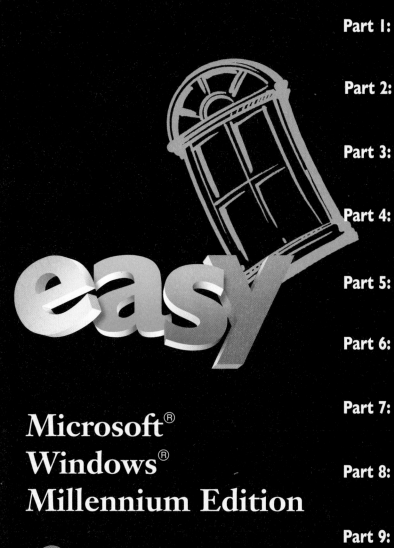

easy

Microsoft®
Windows®
Millennium Edition

See it done

Do it yourself

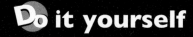

que®

P9-BUH-354

Part ▶ 4: Printing with Windows

Part ▶ 5: Using Windows Accessories

Part ▶ 6: Entertainment

Easy Microsoft® Windows® Millennium Edition
Copyright© 2000 by Que® Corporation

International Standard Book Number: 0-7897-2406-5

Library of Congress Catalog Card Number: 00-102233

Printed in the United States of America

First Printing: August, 2000

02   01   4   3

Trademarks

All terms mentioned in this book that are known to be trademarks or service marks have been appropriately capitalized. Que Corporation cannot attest to the accuracy of this information. Use of a term in this book should not be regarded as affecting the validity of any trademark or service mark.

Microsoft is a registered trademark of Microsoft Corporation.

Windows is a registered trademark of Microsoft Corporation.

Warning and Disclaimer

Every effort has been made to make this book as complete and as accurate as possible, but no warranty or fitness is implied. The information provided is on an "as is" basis. The author and the publisher shall have neither liability nor responsibility to any person or entity with respect to any loss or damages arising from the information contained in this book.

Associate Publisher
Greg Wiegand

Senior Acquisitions Editor
Jenny L. Watson

Development Editor
Todd Brakke

Managing Editor
Thomas Hayes

Project Editor
Tonya R. Simpson

Indexer
Chris Barrick

Proofreader
Benjamin Berg

Technical Editor
Aaron Rogers

Team Coordinator
Sharry Gregory

Interior Designer
Anne Jones

Cover Designer
Anne Jones

Production
Jeannette McKay

About the Author

Shelley O'Hara is the author of more than 90 books, including the best-selling *Easy Windows 2000* and *Easy Windows 98*. She has a B.A. in English from the University of South Carolina and an M.A. in English from the University of Maryland.

Dedication

To my college buddies—Maureen Klimovich (now Cates), Carolyn T. Price (now Minesinger), and Mary Beth Sigmon (now Freeman). Thanks for all the memories!

Acknowledgments

To start, I would like to thank Todd Brakke, development editor. Not only is he so pleasant to work with, but his suggestions helped improve this edition of the book. My thanks also to the tech editor Aaron Rogers, Tonya Simpson, project editor, and Jenny Watson, acquisitions editor.

How to Use This Book

It's as Easy as 1-2-3

Each part of this book is made up of a series of short, instructional lessons, designed to help you understand basic information that you need to get the most out of your computer hardware and software.

 Click: Click the left mouse button once.

 Double-click: Click the left mouse button twice in rapid succession.

 Right-click: Click the right mouse button once.

Pointer Arrow: Highlights an item on the screen you need to point to or focus on in the step or task.

 Selection: Highlights the area onscreen discussed in the step or task.

 Click & Type: Click once where indicated and begin typing to enter your text or data.

 Tips and Warnings give you a heads-up for any extra information you may need while working through the task.

(2) Each task includes a series of quick, easy steps designed to guide you through the procedure.

 **Drag**

Drop

How to Drag: Point to the starting place or object. Hold down the mouse button (right or left per instructions), move the mouse to the new location, then release the button.

(1) Each step is fully illustrated to show you how it looks onscreen.

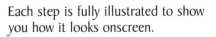
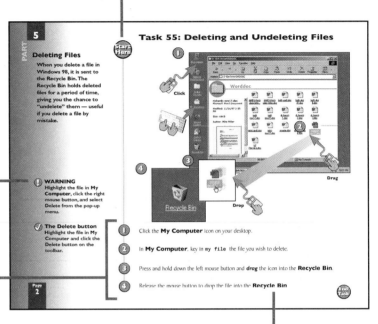

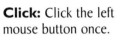 **Task 55: Deleting and Undeleting Files**

Deleting Files

When you delete a file in Windows 98, it is sent to the Recycle Bin. The Recycle Bin holds deleted files for a period of time, giving you the chance to "undelete" them — useful if you delete a file by mistake.

Click

Drag

(!) WARNING Highlight the file in **My Computer**, click the right mouse button, and select Delete from the pop-up menu.

(✓) The Delete button Highlight the file in **My Computer** and click the Delete button on the toolbar.

Drop

(1) Click the **My Computer** icon on your desktop.

(2) In **My Computer**, key in my file the file you wish to delete.

(3) Press and hold down the left mouse button and *drag* the icon into the **Recycle Bin**.

(4) Release the mouse button to drop the file into the **Recycle Bin**.

(3) Items that you select or click in menus, dialog boxes, tabs, and windows are shown in **bold**. Information you type is in a `special font`.

 Next Step: If you see this symbol, it means the task you're working on continues on the next page.

 End Task: Task is complete.

Introduction to Easy Microsoft Windows Millennium Edition

Becoming proficient with a new operating system such as Windows Millennium can seem like a daunting task. There's so much to learn: How do you create and edit documents? How can you customize the desktop? How do you connect to the Internet? Sometimes these questions can seem overwhelming.

That's why *Easy Microsoft Windows Millennium Edition* provides concise, visual, step-by-step instructions for handling all the tasks you'll need to accomplish. You'll learn how to get started in Windows Millennium, how to use applications, how to organize your materials, how to print, how to personalize your system, how to set up programs, how to use Windows accessories, how to maintain your system, how to connect to online services, and more.

You can read this book cover to cover or use it as a reference when you encounter a piece of Windows Millennium that you don't know how to use. Either way, *Easy Microsoft Windows Millennium Edition* lets you see it done and do it yourself.

Tell Us What You Think!

As the reader of this book, *you* are our most important critic and commentator. We value your opinion and want to know what we're doing right, what we could do better, what areas you'd like to see us publish in, and any other words of wisdom you're willing to pass our way.

As an associate publisher for Que, I welcome your comments. You can fax, email, or write me directly to let me know what you did or didn't like about this book—as well as what we can do to make our books stronger.

Please note that I cannot help you with technical problems related to the topic of this book, and that due to the high volume of mail I receive, I might not be able to reply to every message.

When you write, please be sure to include this book's title and author as well as your name and phone or fax number. I will carefully review your comments and share them with the author and editors who worked on the book.

Fax: 317-581-4666

Email: feedback@quepublishing.com

Mail: Associate Publisher
Que Corporation
201 West 103rd Street
Indianapolis, IN 46290 USA

Getting Started

Windows Millennium is the newest version of Windows. Introduced in 2000, this version includes some new features designed to make your computer easier to use. If you purchased a new computer recently, this is the version you most likely have. You can also upgrade to Windows Millennium by purchasing the new version from a retail store or from Microsoft.

You don't need to do anything to start Windows Millennium other than turn on your PC. Windows starts automatically when you turn on your computer, and you see a screen called the *desktop*. The desktop is your starting point. Here you find the key tools for working with your computer. From your Windows desktop, you can open and switch between applications, search for specific folders, print documents, and perform other tasks. This section covers the basics of working with the desktop.

Tasks

Task 1: Displaying the Start Menu

The taskbar, located at the bottom of your screen, contains the **Start** button. Clicking the **Start** button enables you to start applications, open documents you have recently used, customize settings in Windows, get help, and more. You use the **Start** button to begin most tasks in Windows.

✓ **Close the Menu**
If you click the **Start** button by mistake and want to close the **Start** menu without choosing a command, simply click outside the menu or press the **Esc** key.

✓ **Arrow at Bottom?**
If you see an arrow at the bottom of a menu, you are using personalized menus on which only the most frequently used commands are listed. You can click the arrow to display all commands. You can also turn off this feature. See Part 8, "Personalizing Windows."

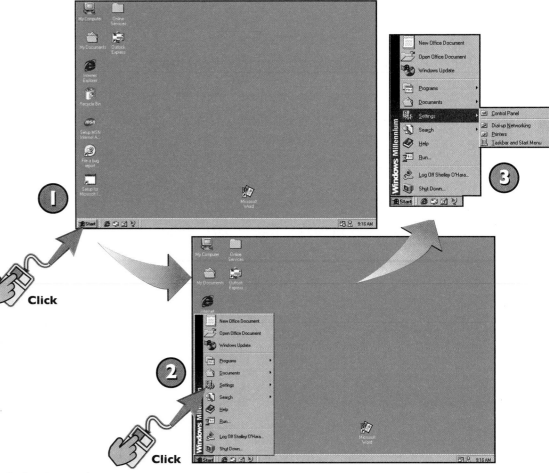

Click

Click

1 Click the **Start** button.

2 Click the menu (marked with an arrow) you want. For example, click **Settings**.

3 You see a list of the commands in that menu. For example, if you click **Settings**, you see commands for Settings.

Task 2: Opening a Window

Start Here

Double-Click ①

②

Windows Millennium displays all its information in onscreen boxes called *windows*. To work with any of the information on your computer, you must know how to display (or open) these windows. Most windows are represented onscreen by small pictures called *icons*. You can double-click an icon to display the contents of the window the icon represents.

✔ **Nothing Happens?**
If nothing happens when you double-click an icon, it might be because you did not click quickly enough or because you single-clicked, moved the mouse, and single-clicked again. You must click twice in rapid succession. A good way to practice using the mouse is to play Solitaire.

① Double-click the **My Computer** icon.

② The contents of this icon are displayed, and a button for the My Computer window appears on the taskbar.

✔ **Single-Click**
If your desktop is set up as a Web desktop (covered later in this book), you can simply single-click to open an icon.

Task 3: Closing a Window

You close a window after you finish working with it and its contents. Too many open windows clutter the desktop and taskbar as well as slow down your computer.

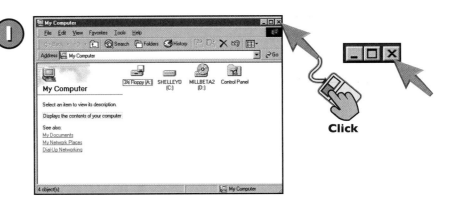

Click

✓ Use the Control Menu

The **Control** menu, located in the upper-left corner of the title bar, contains commands related to the open window, such as **Restore, Move, Size, Close**, and so on. To close the window via the **Control** menu, click the **Control Menu** icon, and then choose **Close** from the menu. Alternatively, you can press **Alt+F4**.

✓ Check the Taskbar

You can tell which windows you have open by looking at the taskbar.

Click the **Close** button (the button marked with an × in the top-right corner of the **My Computer** window).

The window closes, and the button for the window no longer appears in the taskbar.

Task 4: Minimizing a Window

You can reduce (minimize) a window so that it is still available as a taskbar button but is not displayed on the desktop. You might want to minimize a window to temporarily move it out of your way but keep it active for later use.

1 Click the **Minimize** button (marked with a line) in the window you want to minimize.

2 The window disappears from the desktop, but a button for this window remains on the taskbar.

Task 5: Maximizing a Window

You can enlarge (maximize) a window so that it fills the entire screen. Doing so gives you as much room as possible to work in that window.

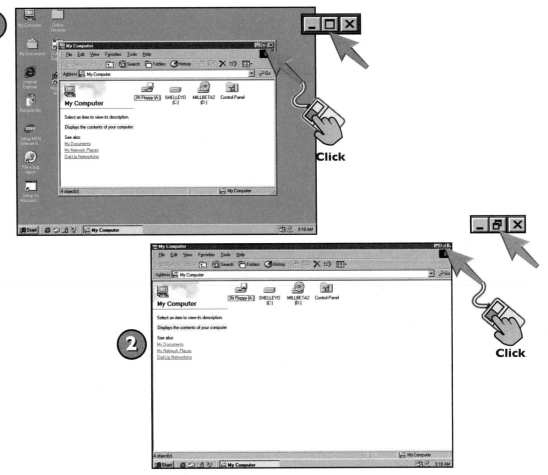

① Click the **Maximize** button (the button marked with a square).

② The window enlarges to fill the screen, and the **Maximize** button changes to the **Restore** button explained in Task 6.

Task 6: Restoring a Window

Start Here

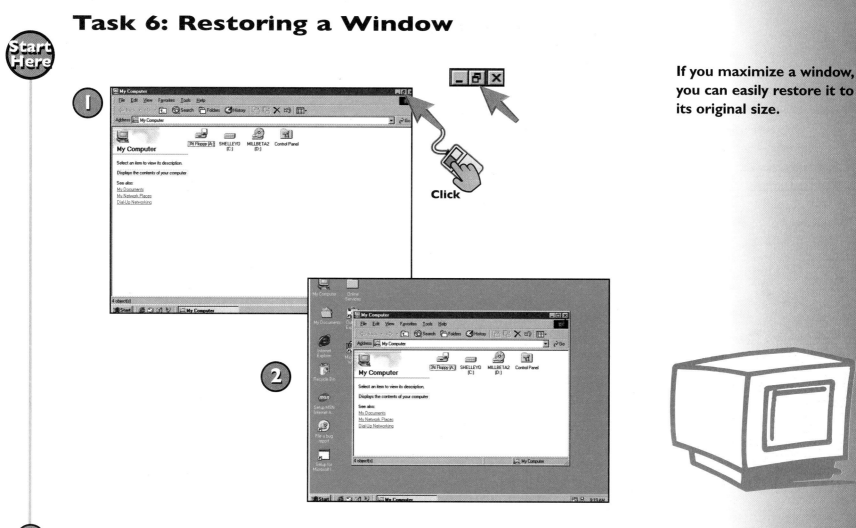

If you maximize a window, you can easily restore it to its original size.

Click

1. In a maximized window, click the **Restore** button (the button marked with two boxes).

2. The window is restored to its original size.

End Task

Task 7: Moving a Window

As you open more applications, folders, shortcuts, and so on, you'll need more room to display these windows on the desktop. You can easily move them around so you can see more open windows at one time.

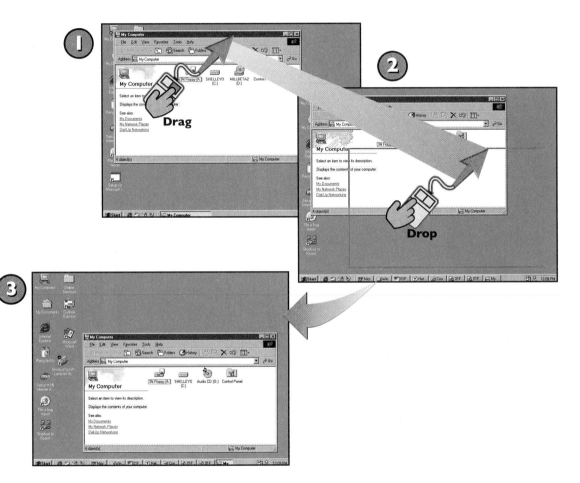

Drag

Drop

(✓) **The Title Bar**

Be sure to point to the colored area of the title bar. If you point to any other area, you might resize the window instead of move it.

1 To move an open window, point to its title bar. Click and hold down the mouse button.

2 Drag the window to a new position. You can see the border of the window as you drag.

3 Release the mouse button. The window and its contents appear in the new location.

End Task

Task 8: Resizing a Window

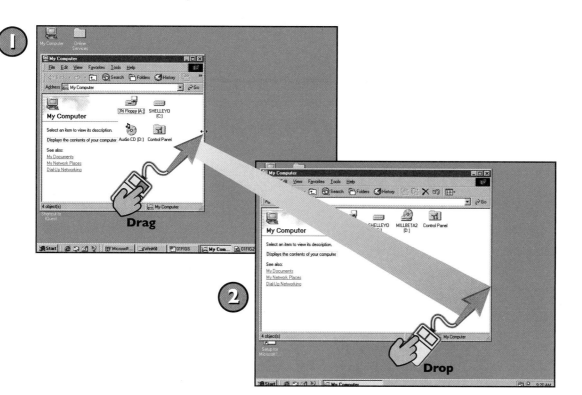

Drag

Drop

In addition to being able to move a window, you can resize a window to whatever size you want. Resizing windows is helpful if you want to view more than one window at the same time.

✓ **No Borders?**
You cannot resize a maximized window. If you don't see borders, you cannot resize the window. If you want to resize the window, simply click the **Restore** button, and then resize it.

✓ **Resize from Corner**
You can drag a corner of the window to proportionally resize both dimensions (height and width) at the same time.

1 Point to any window border. You should see a double-headed arrow pointing out the directions in which you can size the window.

2 Drag the border to resize the window, and then release the mouse button. The window is now resized.

Task 9: Scrolling a Window

If a window is too small to show all its contents, vertical *scrollbars* appear along the edges of the window. You can use these bars to scroll through the window to see the other contents.

Start Here

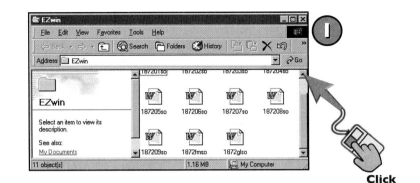
Click

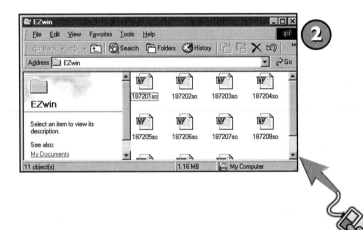
Click

✓ **Click for Fast Scrolling**
You can click anywhere in the scrollbar to jump in that direction to another part of the window. You can also click the scroll box to scroll quickly through the window.

✓ **Mouse Scrolling**
If you have a new computer, you might have a mouse with the rotating button between the left and right buttons. You can use this button to scroll windows up and down.

1 Click the up arrow to scroll up through the window.

2 Click the down arrow to scroll down through the window.

End Task

Task 10: Arranging Windows on the Desktop

Start Here

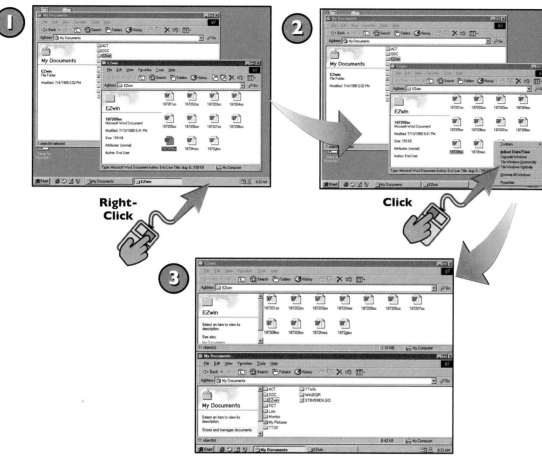

Right-Click

Click

As you work, you will often have several windows open on the desktop at one time. The windows probably overlap each other, which can make it difficult to find what you want. To make your work easier and more efficient, Windows enables you to arrange the windows on the desktop in several different ways.

✓ **Right-Click a Blank Part**
When choosing a window arrangement, be sure to right-click on a blank area of the taskbar, not on a button.

✓ **Undo**
Undo the arrangement by right-clicking again and choosing **Undo**.

✓ **Select a Window**
To work in any of the open windows, click the desired window to make it active. The active window moves to the front of the stack, and its title bar changes to a different color.

① With multiple windows on the desktop, right-click a blank area of the taskbar.

② Click the arrangement you want.

③ Windows arranges the windows; here they are tiled horizontally.

End Task

Task 11: Using Menus

Although you can perform many tasks by clicking the mouse on different onscreen objects, you must choose commands to perform the majority of Windows tasks. Commands are organized in menus to make them easy to find. Most windows contain menu bars that list the available menus; each menu then contains a group of related commands.

✓ See an Arrow?

Selecting a command that is followed by an arrow will display a *submenu* (a menu within a menu). Clicking a command that is followed by an ellipsis will display a dialog box (covered in Task 13, "Using a Dialog Box").

✓ Close a Menu

To close a menu without making a selection, you can also press the **Esc** key on your keyboard or click outside the menu.

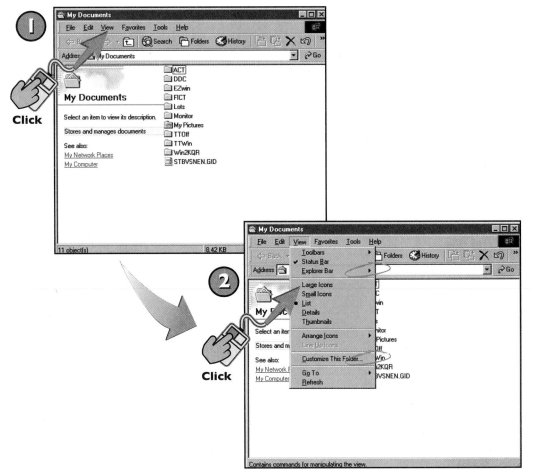

Click

Click

1 In the window or program, click the menu name (in this case, the menu name is **View**).

2 Click the command you want.

Task 12: Using Shortcut Menus

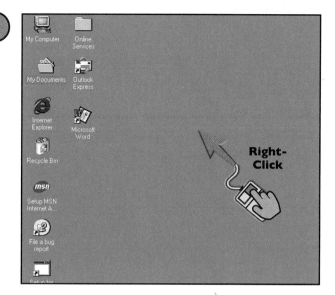

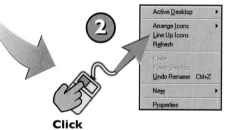

Shortcut menus, also called *quick menus* and *pop-up menus,* provide common commands related to the selected item. You can, for example, quickly copy and paste, create a new folder, move a file, or rearrange icons using a shortcut menu.

① Right-click the item for which you want to display a shortcut menu. For example, right-click any blank part of the desktop.

② Click the command you want in the shortcut menu.

✓ Menus Vary
Different shortcut menus appear depending on what you're pointing to when you right-click the mouse.

Task 13: Using a Dialog Box

When you choose certain commands, a dialog box prompts you for additional information about how to carry out the command. Dialog boxes are used throughout Windows; luckily, all dialog boxes have common elements, and all aretreated in a similar way. This task uses the **Display Properties** dialog box to show many options. You can display this by right-clicking a blank part of the desktop and selecting **Properties**.

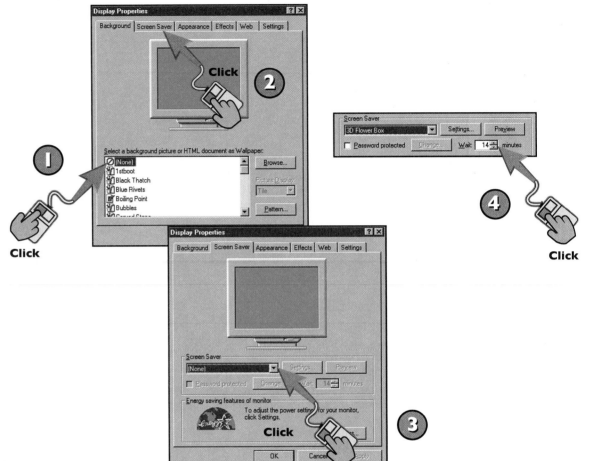

Click

Click

Click

(1) To use a list box, scroll through the list and click the item you want to select.

(2) To view a tab, click it.

(3) To use a drop-down list box, click the arrow, and then select the desired item from the list.

(4) To use a spin box, click the arrows to increment or decrement the value, or type a value in the text box.

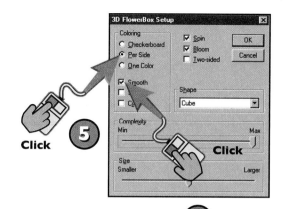

Click ⑤ **Click**

⑥

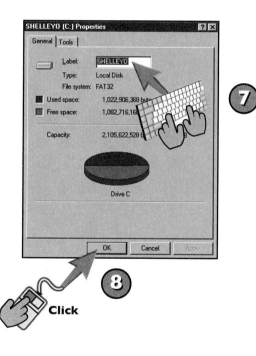

⑦

Click ⑧

⑤ Click a radio button to activate it.

⑥ Click a check box to select it (or to deselect a check box that is already checked).

⑦ Type an entry in a text box.

⑧ After you make your selections, click the **OK** button.

✓ **Radio Buttons and Check Boxes**
Dialog boxes contain various types of elements, including radio buttons and check boxes. You can choose only one radio button within a group of radio buttons; choosing a second option deselects the first. However, you can select multiple check boxes within a group of check boxes.

Task 14: Starting an Application from the Start Menu

Most of the time you spend using your computer will be with an application. An *application* is a computer program you use to perform some task. For example, a word processing application is used to create letters, reports, and other typed documents. You can start an application in any number of ways, including from the **Start** menu. When you install a new Windows application, that program's installation procedure will set up a program folder and program icon on the **Start** menu.

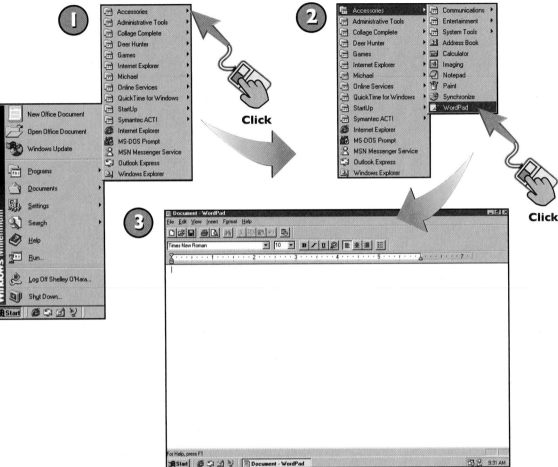

Start Here

Click

Click

✓ Program Not Listed?
If you don't see your program icon listed, you can easily add programs to the **Start** menu. For more information about how to handle this, see Part 10, "Setting Up Programs."

1 Click **Start**, **Programs** and select the program group that contains the application you want to start (in this case, **Accessories**).

2 Click the application you want to start (**WordPad** is selected here).

3 The application opens in its own window.

End Task

Task 15: Closing an Application

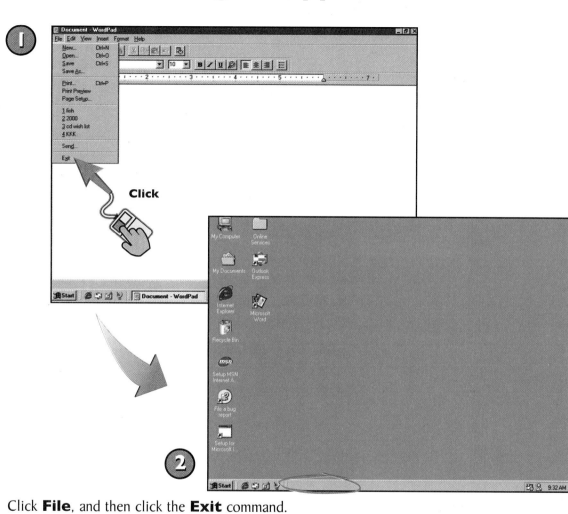

Click

When you finish working in an application, close it to free system memory. Too many open applications can tax your system's memory and slow the computer's processes, such as saving, printing, switching between applications, and so on.

More Ways
To close an application, you can also press **Alt+F4** or click the **Close** button in the application's title bar.

WARNING!
If you have not saved a file and choose to close that file's application, a message box appears asking if you want to save the file. If you do, click **Yes;** if not, click **No.** If you want to return to the document, click **Cancel.**

① Click **File**, and then click the **Exit** command.

② The program closes. Notice that the taskbar button for WordPad has disappeared.

Task 16: Looking Up a Help Topic

You can use the Windows **Help** command to get help on common topics. You can select from a list of topics, as covered here.

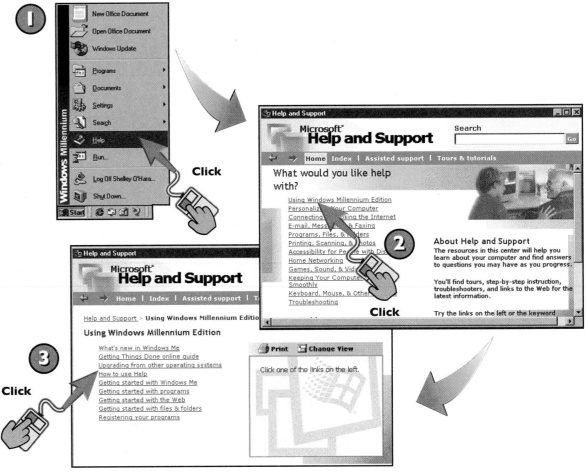

Click

Click

Click

---

① Click **Start**, **Help**.

(✓) **Definitions**
You can click any of the underlined text in the help area to display a definition of that term or to display related help information.

② Click the topic you want help on.

③ Continue clicking topics until you find the exact help topic you need, and then click that help topic.

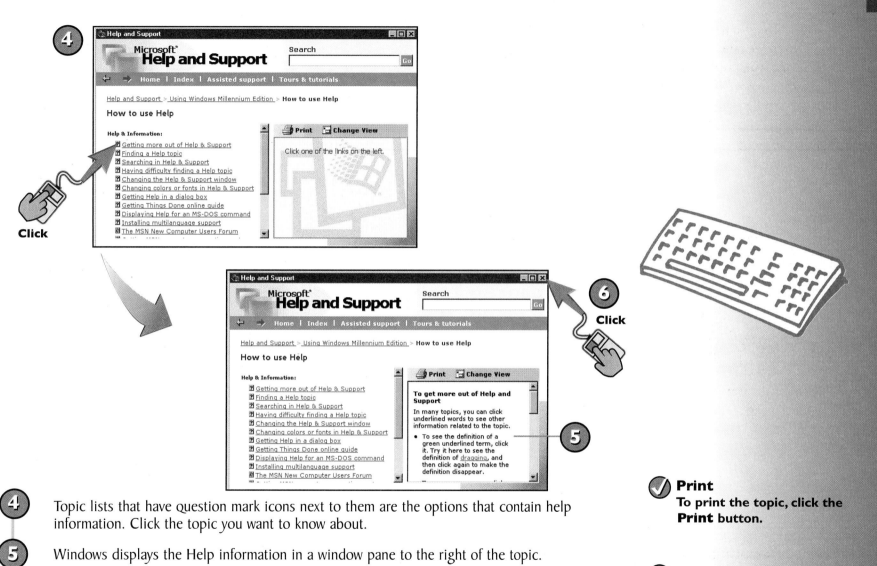

Click

Click

6

5

(4) Topic lists that have question mark icons next to them are the options that contain help information. Click the topic you want to know about.

(5) Windows displays the Help information in a window pane to the right of the topic.

(6) When finished, click the **Close (X)** button to close the Help window.

✅ **Print**
To print the topic, click the **Print** button.

✅ **Go Back**
You can click the **Back** button to go back to the previous help page.

End
Task

Task 17: Looking Up a Help Topic in the Index

If you want to find help on a specific topic, such as storing files by size or editing text, use the *index*. Topics are listed in alphabetical order. You can quickly scroll to see topics of interest.

Start Here

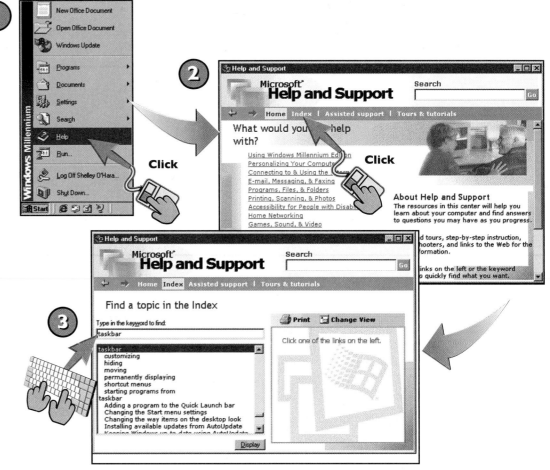

Click

Click

1. Click the **Start** button, and then select **Help**.

2. Click the **Index** button in the **Help and Support** dialog box.

3. Type the topic for which you want to find help. The list below the text field jumps to the topic you type.

Next Step

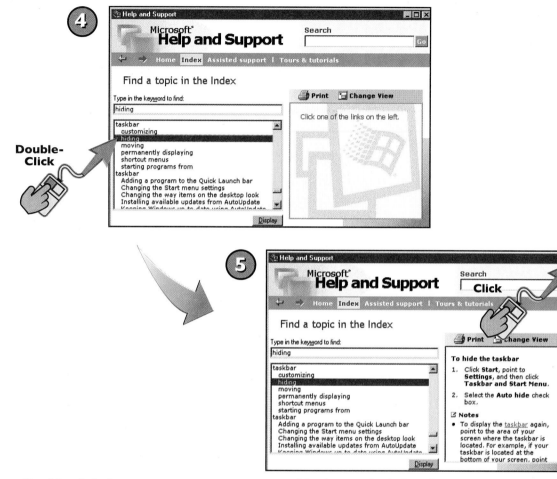

Double-Click

Double-click the topic you want to review, and look over the help information.

Click the **Close** button.

Help Works the Same
Windows Help works in the same way throughout most Windows applications. If you master Help basics, you can apply these same skills to other Windows-based programs.

End Task

Task 18: Searching for a Help Topic

If you don't find the topic in the list or index, try searching for it. Windows will display a list of topics that contains what you are looking for; you can then select the one you want.

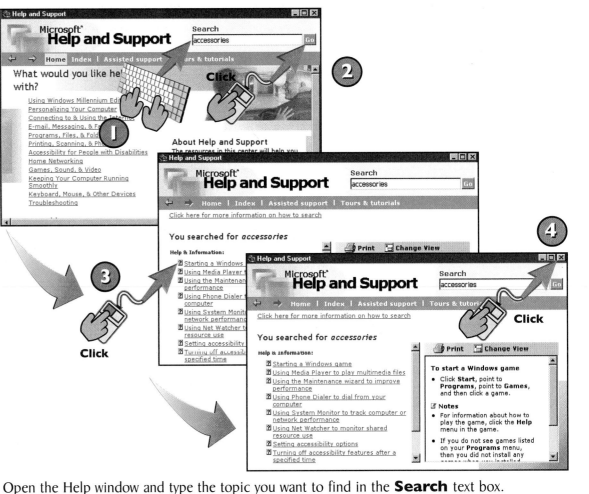

① Open the Help window and type the topic you want to find in the **Search** text box.

② Click **GO** to execute a search on that topic.

③ You see a list of matching topics. Click the topic you want to review.

④ Review the help information, and then click the **Close (X)** button.

Task 19: Getting Context-Sensitive Help

Start Here

1

Display Properties

Background | Screen Saver | Appearance | Effects | Web | Settings

Select a background picture or HTML document as Wallpaper:

(None)
1stboot
Black Thatch
Blue Rivets
Boiling Point
Bubbles

Browse...

Picture Display:
Tile

Pattern...

Right-Click

Display Properties

Background | Screen Saver | Appearance | Effects | Web | Settings

Select a background picture or HTML document as Wallpaper:

(None)
1stboot
Black Thatch
Blue Rivets
Boiling Point
Bubbles

Browse

What's This?

Picture Display:
Tile

Pattern...

Cancel | Apply

Click

2

Display Properties

Background | Screen Saver | Appearance | Effects | Web | Settings

Select a background picture or HTML doc...

(None)
1stboot
Black Thatch
Blue Rivets
Boiling Point
Bubbles

Click this to search for wallpaper on other drives or in other folders. You can use many different file types as wallpaper, including: .bmp, .gif, .jpg, .dib, .png, and .htm files.

OK | Cancel | Apply

Click

3

When you open a dialog box, you might not know what each of the options does. If you have a question about an option, there is a way you can view a description of that option by following the steps in this task.

1 In a dialog box, right-click the option you want help on.

2 In the menu that appears, click the **What's This?** command.

3 After you review the material in the pop-up explanation, click anywhere within the dialog box to close the pop-up box.

End Task

Task 20: Restarting the Computer

Sometimes you will need to restart your computer. You might do this if the computer gets stuck or if you make changes and need to restart to put the changes into effect.

Start Here

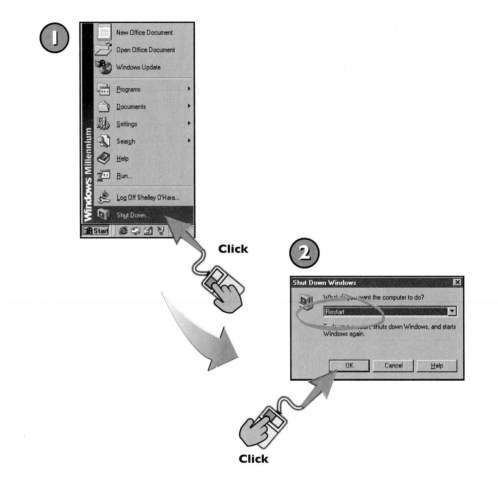

Click

Click

✓ **Standby**
To put the computer on standby to conserve power, select the **Standby** option, and then click **OK**. Standby turns off your monitor and hard disk but keeps all open applications stored in memory.

1 If possible, close all open programs. Then click **Start**, **Shut Down**.

2 Select **Restart** from the drop-down list, and click **OK**.

End Task

Task 21: Shutting Down the Computer

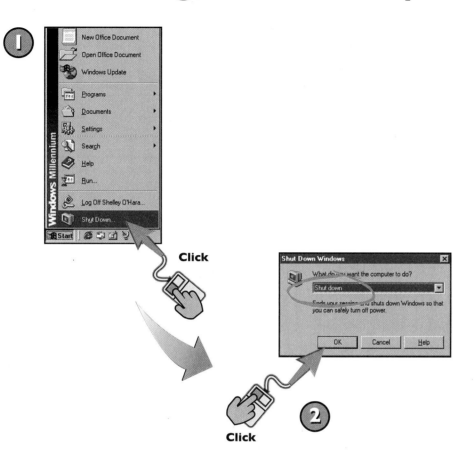

Click

Click

If you turn off the power to your computer before you properly shut the computer down, you could lose valuable data or damage an open file. Windows provides a safe shutdown feature that checks for open programs and files, warns you to save unsaved files, and prepares the program for you to turn off your computer. You should always shut down when you are finished using your computer.

1. After you've closed down all open programs, click **Start**, **Shut Down**.

2. Select **Shut down** from the drop-down list, and click **OK**.

 Cancel Shutdown
If you don't want to shut down Windows, click the **Cancel** button.

PART 2

Working with Disks, Folders, and Files

One part of working with Windows is learning how to work with the documents you save and store on your system. Each time you save a document (a letter, worksheet, or database), that information is saved as a file on your hard disk. You assign both a specific place for the file and a name.

To keep your files organized, you can set up folders. If your hard drive is like a big filing cabinet then folders are like drawers. Each folder can hold files or other folders. You can open and close folders, view a folder's contents, copy and move folders, and create or delete folders.

The more you work on your computer, the more files and folders you add. After a while, your computer will become cluttered, and you'll need a way to keep these files organized. Windows provides features that can help you find, organize, and manage your files. You can copy files, move files, delete unnecessary files, and more.

Tasks

Task 1: Opening Folder Windows

Folders contain files, programs, or other items that you can use to do work in Windows. You can display the contents of a folder to work with the files—move a file, create a shortcut icon, start a program, and so on.

✅ Use Links
Millennium displays, by default, an information pane along the left. You can get information about a selected item. This area also displays related links. Click the link to go to that folder.

✅ Change the View
You can select how the contents of a folder are displayed. See Tasks 4, "Changing How the Contents of a Window Are Displayed," and 6, "Sorting the Contents of a Window," later in this part.

✅ No Files Appear
The first time you open My Computer you might not see any files listed. Click the Show Files link to display files.

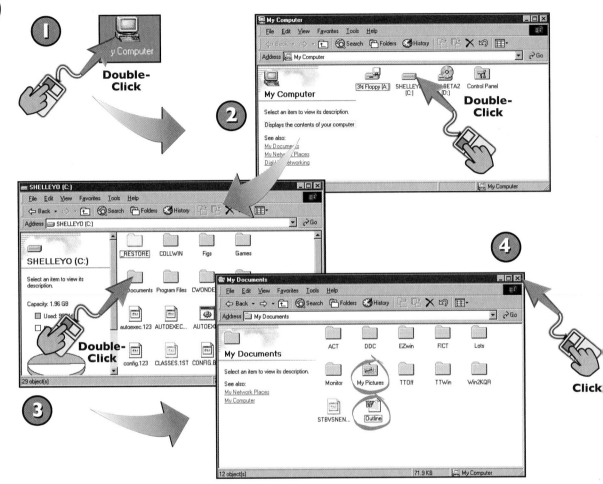

(1) Double-click the **My Computer** icon on the desktop.

(2) Double-click the icon representing your hard drive (usually **C:**).

(3) Each folder icon represents a folder on your hard drive. Double-click any folder.

(4) Each folder icon represents groups of files and folders. Each page icon represents a document (file). Click the **Close** button to close the window.

Task 2: Using the My Documents Folder

Start Here

① Double-Click

②

```
My Documents
File  Edit  View  Favorites  Tools  Help
← Back → ⯅ ↰ ☰ Search ☐ Folders ❀ History │ ⬚ ⬚ ✕ ⟲ ▦ ▾
Address ☐ My Documents                              ▾ ⬀ Go

    [icon]              ☐ ACT
                        ☐ DDC
My Documents            ☐ EZwin
                        ☐ L
Select an item to view its description.  ☐ Mo...
                        ☐ My Pictures
Stores and manages documents  ☐ TTOff
                        ☐ TTWin
See also:               ☐ Win2KQR
My Network Places       ▤ STBVSNEN.GIF
My Computer             ☷ Outline

12 object(s)                    71.9 KB    ☐ My Computer
```
Double-Click

③

```
EZwin                                          _ ▢ ✕
File  Edit  View  Favorites  Tools  Help
← Back → ⯅ ↰ ☰ Search ☐ Folders ❀ History │ ⬚ ⬚ ✕ ⟲ ▦ ▾
Address ☐ EZwin                                 ▾ ⬀ Go

    [icon]     ₩    ₩    ₩    ₩    ₩
             187201so 187202so 187203so 187204so 187205so
EZwin
             ₩    ₩    ₩    ₩    ₩
Select an item to view its description.  187206so 187207so 187208so 187209so 1872fmso
See also:
My Documents   ₩
My Network Places  1872glso
My Computer

11 object(s)                    1.16 MB    ☐ My Computer
```
Click

① Double-click the **My Documents** icon on the desktop.

② If you have added any folders to this folder, you see them listed. Double-click any folder to display its contents.

③ You see the contents of this folder. Click the **Close** button to close the window.

To help you keep your documents organized, Windows sets up a special folder called **My Documents.** You can view the contents using the **My Documents** icon on the desktop. When you organize your documents, it's a good idea to use the **My Documents** folder, creating subfolders (a folder within a folder) within this main folder to store your work.

✓ **Add Folders**
You can add folders to the **My Documents** folder. To do so, see Task 9, "Creating a Folder."

✓ **Shortcuts**
Many programs include a shortcut button to the **My Documents** folder. You can click this button to quickly change to this folder.

End Task

Task 3: Using the My Pictures Folder

Windows also sets up another special folder within the **My Documents** folder. This folder is useful for storing pictures—graphic files from a scanner or camera.

Start Here

① Double-Click

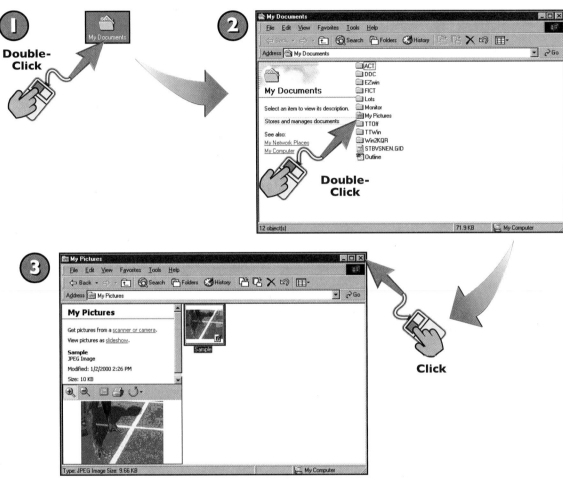

Double-Click

Click

✓ **Thumbnail View**
You should see the contents in **Thumbnail** view, which shows miniature pictures of each graphic file. You can change to another view (or switch to **Thumbnail** if you don't see this view) using the **Views** command or button. See the next task.

① Double-click the **My Documents** icon on the desktop.

② Double-click the folder for **My Pictures**.

③ You see the contents of this folder. Click the **Close** button to close the window.

Task 4: Changing How the Contents of a Window Are Displayed

Start Here

1 Click

You can view the contents of a window in a variety of ways. Windows uses large icons to display the contents of most windows. If you want to see more of a window's contents at one time, you can change the view to **Small Icons** or **List**. You can also display such details about an item as its type, its size, and the date it was last modified. Changing the way a window displays its contents can make it easier to find what you need.

2

1 In the window you want to change, click the **View** menu, and then select the view you want.

2 The window displays the contents in that view (in this case, the **Details** view).

Task 5: Using the Toolbar Buttons in a File Window

Each window, whether it's a file or folder window, includes a toolbar that you can use to navigate from folder to folder and to make changes to the files and folders.

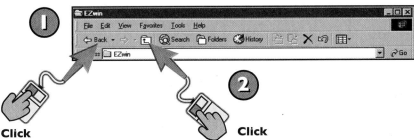

Click   **Click**

Click

Click the **Back** button to go back to a previously viewed page.

Click the **Up** button to display the next level up in the folder structure.

Click the **Forward** button to go forward (after going back) to a previously viewed page.

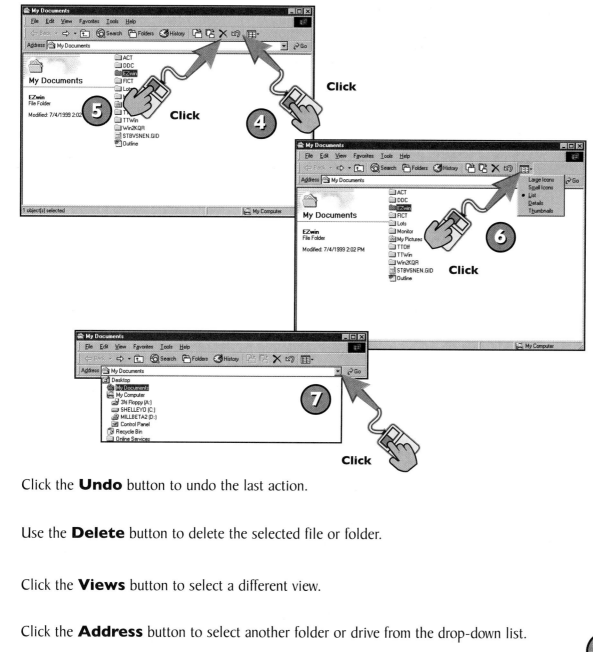

Click

Click

Click

Click

Click

Search and Folders
You can find information on using Search in Task 23, "Finding Files and Folders."

Button Name
If you aren't sure what a toolbar button does, put the pointer on the button. A ToolTip name pops up, explaining its function.

4 Click the **Undo** button to undo the last action.

5 Use the **Delete** button to delete the selected file or folder.

6 Click the **Views** button to select a different view.

7 Click the **Address** button to select another folder or drive from the drop-down list.

End Task

Task 6: Sorting the Contents of a Window

You sort the contents of a window so that you can more easily find the files you want. Windows enables you to arrange the files in a folder by name, type, date, and size. Sorting the files is even easier if you choose to view them by the file details first. You can sort files viewed as large or small icons or as a list.

Start Here

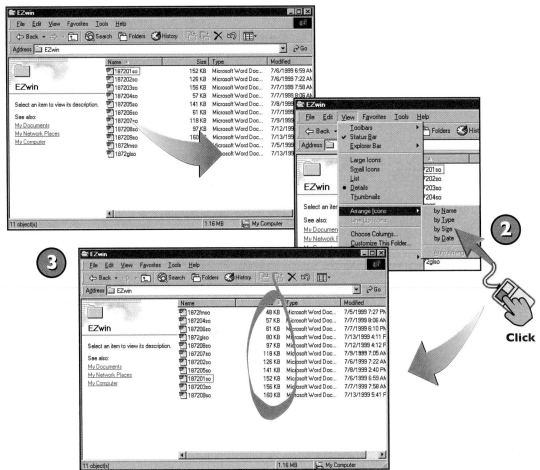

Click

✓ Sort Orders

You can also sort by name in alphabetical order, by file type, or by date from oldest to most recent by choosing the appropriate command from the **Arrange Icons** submenu. You can also click the column header in the **Details** view to sort by that column.

✓ My Computer Sorts

If you are working in the **My Computer** window, you have different options for arranging the icons. You can arrange by type, size, drive letter, or free space.

① Open the window you want to sort. In this case, the window is displayed in **Detail** view so that you can see the results of sorting by different columns.

② Click **View**, **Arrange Icons** and choose the sort order you want (in this case, **by Size**).

③ Windows sorts the files in the selected order. For example, this view shows the files sorted by size from the smallest to largest.

End Task

Task 7: Displaying the Folders Bar

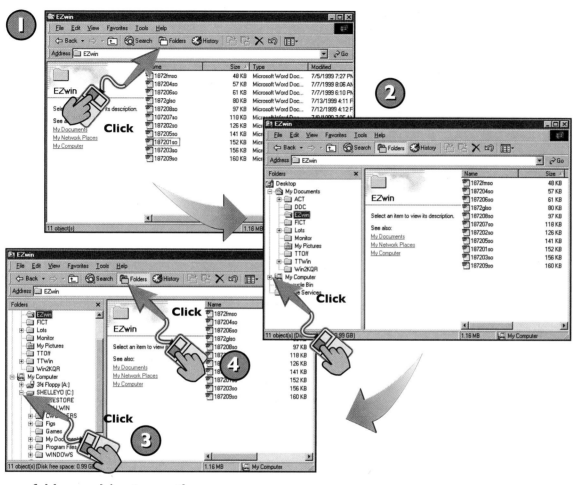

If you want to see a <$selecting;folders;Folders bar>hierarchical listing of all the folders on your system, you can display this list in the **Folders** bar. You might prefer this view when making changes to your files, especially moving and copying files from one

✓ **Navigate Folders**
You can select folders in the **Folders** bar by clicking the folder you want. The right pane then shows the contents of the selected folder.

✓ **Windows Explorer**
You can use Windows Explorer in much the same way you use the **My Computer** window: to copy and move folders, to create and rename folders, to view details, and so on. Basically, Windows Explorer is a file window with the **Folders** bar displayed. Click **Start, Programs,** and then **Windows Explorer** to use this feature.

1 folder or drive to another.
In the window you want to view, click the **Folders** button.

2 You see the **Folders** bar listing the main icons on the desktop. Click the plus sign next to **My Computer**.

3 You see the drives. Click the plus sign next to your hard drive to view the folders it contains.

4 To close the **Folders** bar, click the **Folders** button again.

Task 8: Changing the Folder Options

By default, Windows displays related links in the information pane of the window (Web content) and opens each new folder or drive in the same window. You can choose to display the contents of a window as *links* (single-clicking a link opens that item), which makes working with that window similar to browsing the Internet or an *intranet* (an internal network set up like the Internet). With a single click, you can open files, folders, or drives.

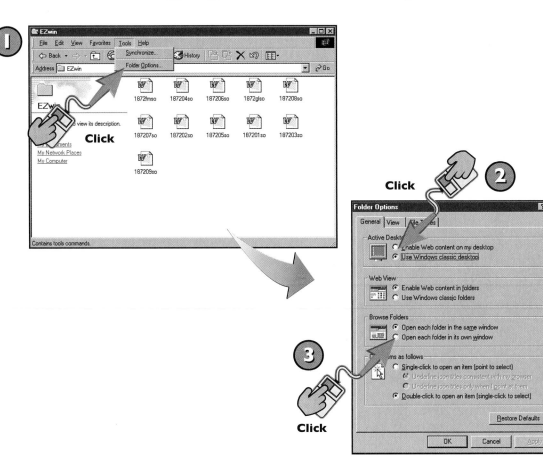

✓ **Classic Style**

To use the Classic style, open the **Tools** menu and choose the **Folder Options** command. Select **Use Windows classic folders,** and click **OK.**

① Click **Tools**, and then select the **Folder Options** command.

② To use Web view, click **Enable Web content on my desktop**.

③ To open a folder in separate windows, click **Open each folder in its own window**.

Folder Options dialog box

Folder Options ? X

General | View | File Types |

Active Desktop
- ○ Enable Web content on my desktop
- ◉ Use Windows classic desktop

Web View
- ◉ Enable Web content in folders
- ○ Use Windows classic folders

Browse Folders
- ◉ Open each folder in the same window
- ○ Open each folder in its own window

Click items as follows
- ◉ Single-click to open an item (point to select)
  - ◉ Underline icon titles consistent with my browser
  - ○ Underline icon titles only when I point at them
- ○ Double-click to open an item (single-click to select)

[Restore Defaults]

(4)

[OK] [Cancel] [Apply]

Click

(5)

Click

EZwin

File Edit View Favorites Tools Help

⇐ Back ▾ ⇒ ▾ 🔄 | 🔍 Search 📁 Folders 🕓 History | 📋 📑 ✕ ↻ | ▦ ▾

Address 🗀 EZwin ▾ 🔗 Go

EZwin

Select an item to view its description.

See also:
My Documents
My Network Places
My Computer

1872fmso 187204so 187206so 1872qlso 187208so
187207so 187202so 187205so 187201so 187203so
187209so

(6)

11 object(s) | 1.16 MB | 🖳 My Computer

---

(4) To single-click rather than double-click to open an item, select **Single-click to open an item**.

(5) Click the **OK** button.

(6) If you selected single-click, the contents of the window are displayed as links. Click any item to display its contents.

✓ **Single-Click Files**
If you select **Single-click to open an item** in the **Click items as follows** area, the contents of the window are displayed as links. Single-click any item to display its contents.

✓ **Go Back to Defaults**
To return to the default settings for the folder options, display the **Folder Options** dialog box, and then click the **Restore Defaults** button. Finally, click **OK.**

✓ **Shortcut**
You can turn on and off desktop items using the **Active Desktop** menu. Right-click a blank part of the desktop, and then select **Active Desktop.**

Task 9: Creating a Folder

Working with your files is easier if you group related files into folders. For example, you might want to create a folder for all your word processing documents or for your budgets. Creating a folder enables you to keep your documents separated from the program's files so you can easily find your document files.

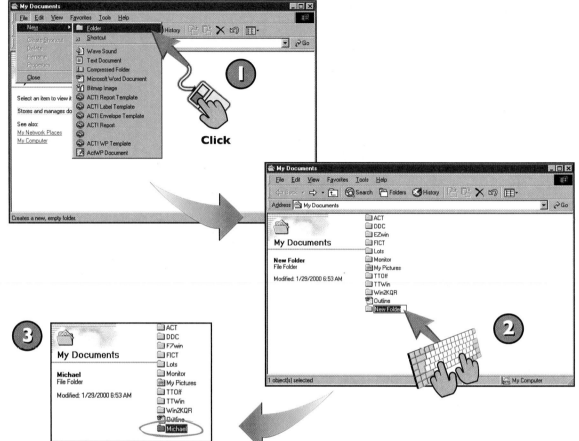

Click

✓ **Delete a Folder**
If you change your mind about the new folder, you can always delete it. To delete the folder, select it, and then press the **Delete** key on your keyboard. Click the **Yes** button to confirm the deletion.

✓ **Folder Name**
The folder name can contain as many as 255 characters and can include spaces. You cannot include these characters:

| ? / : " * < > \

(1) Open **My Documents** and click **File, New, Folder**.

(2) The new folder appears in the window, and the name is highlighted. Type a new name and press **Enter**.

(3) The folder is added.

Task 10: Copying Folders

Start Here

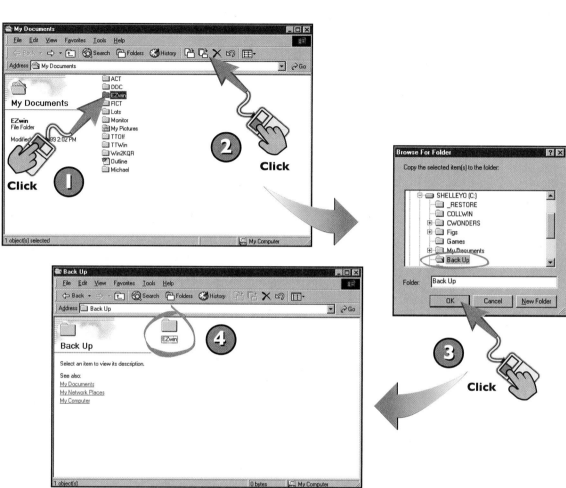

Windows makes it easy for you to copy a folder and its contents and then paste them in a new location. For example, you can copy a folder to a floppy disk to use as a backup or to move to another computer. You can also copy a folder and its contents to another location on the hard drive if, for example, you want to revise the original file for a different use.

✓ **Use Commands**
You can use the **Edit** menu and **Copy** command to copy a folder. Move to the drive or folder window where you want to paste the folder, and select **Edit**, **Paste**. You can also right-click a blank part of the window and select the **Copy** and **Paste** commands.

✓ **Drag a Copy**
You can copy a folder by opening both the window that contains the folder (the source) and the window to which you want to copy the folder (the destination). Click the folder in the source window and drag it to the destination window.

① Click the folder you want to copy.

② Click the **Copy To** button.

③ Expand the folder listing until you can select the drive and folder you want, and click **OK**.

④ Windows copies the new folder and its contents to this location.

Task 11: Moving Folders

You can move a folder and its contents to another folder or to a disk so that you can reorganize your folder structure. For example, you might want to move all related files and folders to the same place on your hard drive so you can find them quickly and easily.

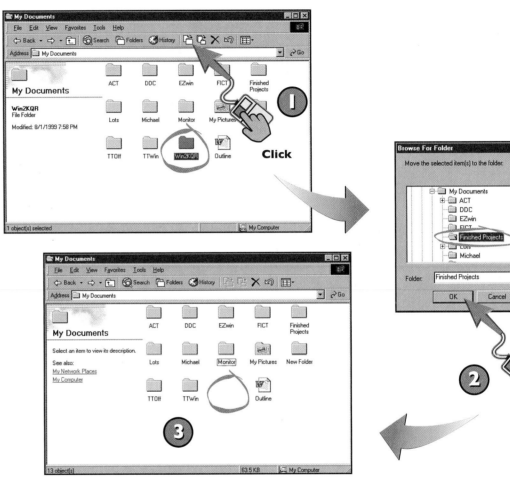

Click

Click

✅ **Drag and Drop**
You can also display the **Folders** bar and drag a folder from the pane on the right to the folder list on the left.

✅ **Main Drives**
You can find the main drives on your computer within the **My Computer** icon. Click the plus sign next to this icon, and then expand the drive listing by clicking the plus sign next to the drive.

✅ **Undo Move**
You can select the **Undo** command from the **Edit** menu to undo the move if you change your mind.

1 Select the folder you want to move, and click the **Move To** button.

2 Expand the folder listing until you see the drive and folder you want. When the folder or drive is selected, click **OK**.

3 Windows moves the folder and its contents to this location.

End Task

Task 12: Renaming Folders

Start Here

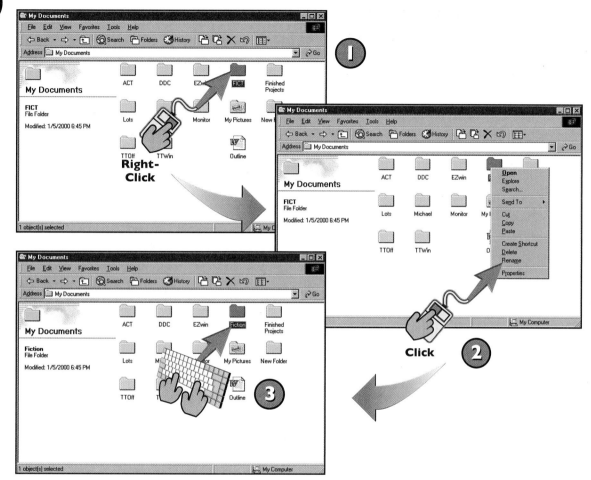

Right-Click

Click

As you add more and more folders and files to your computer, you will eventually need to rearrange and reorganize them. In addition to needing to know how to move folders, you'll need to know how to rename them (for example, in case you want to give a folder a more descriptive name). Fortunately, Windows Millennium lets you easily rename folders.

1. Display the folder you want to rename, and right-click it to bring up a quick menu.

2. Click the **Rename** command.

3. Type the new name and press **Enter**. The folder is renamed.

✓ **Folder Names**
Folder names and filenames can contain as many as 255 characters, including spaces. You also can include letters, numbers, and other symbols on your keyboard, except the following:

| ? / : " * < > \

✓ **Single-Click Renaming**
Click the folder once to select it, and then single-click within the name to edit the name.

End Task

Task 13: Deleting Folders

You can delete folders when you no longer need them. When you delete a folder from your hard drive, you also delete its contents. Windows Millennium places deleted folders in the Recycle Bin. You can restore deleted items from the Recycle Bin if you realize you have placed items there by accident.

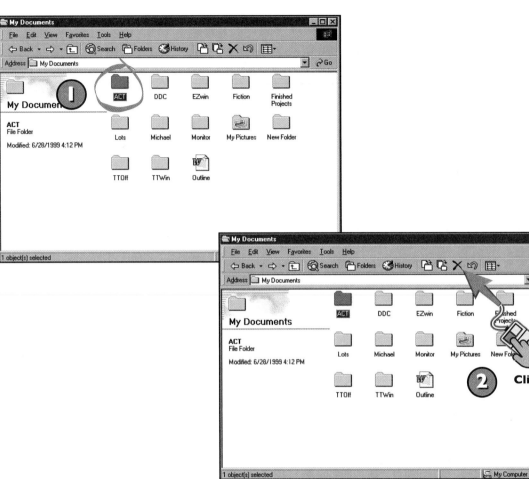

✅ **Cancel Deletion**
If you change your mind about deleting the folder, click the **No** button in the **Confirm Folder Delete** dialog box. Alternatively, undo the deletion by selecting the **Edit Undo** command.

 Select the folder you want to delete.

2 Click the **Delete** button.

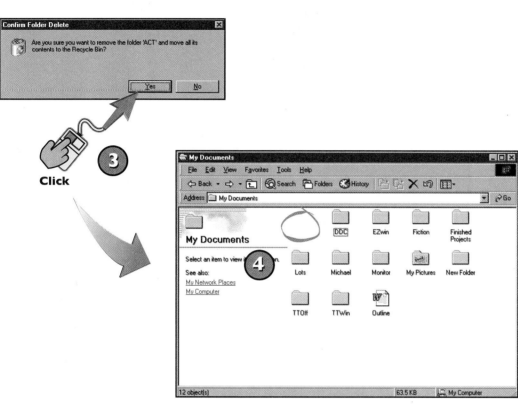

Confirm Folder Delete

Are you sure you want to remove the folder 'ACT' and move all its contents to the Recycle Bin?

Yes | No

Click

③

My Documents

File Edit View Favorites Tools Help

⇐ Back ▾ ⇒ ▾ ⬆ | ◎ Search 🗀 Folders ⏱ History | 🗂 🖳 ✕ ⏪ | ▦▾

Address 🗀 My Documents | ∂Go

My Documents

Select an item to view i...

See also:
My Network Places
My Computer

④

DDC   EZwin   Fiction   Finished Projects

Lots   Michael   Monitor   My Pictures   New Folder

TTOff   TTWin   Outline

12 object(s) | 63.5 KB | 🖳 My Computer

③ Click the **Yes** button.

④ The folder is deleted.

End Task

⚠ WARNING
When you delete a folder from a floppy drive, that item does not land in the Recycle Bin; it is immediately deleted from your system.

Task 14: Selecting a Single File

When you want to work on files (copy, move, print, delete, and so on), you start by selecting the files you want. Selecting a single file is simple.

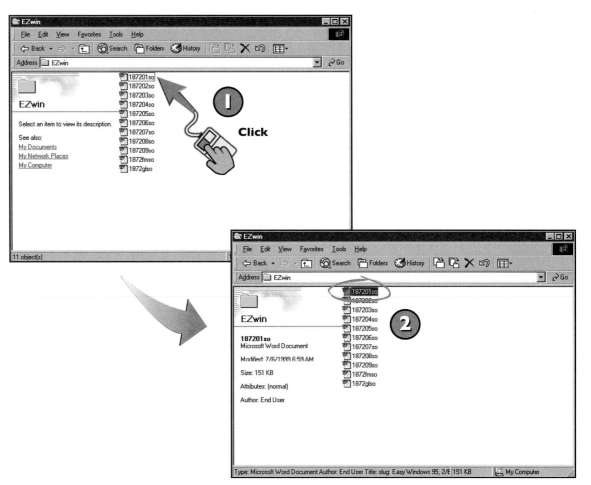

① Click the file you want to work with.

② That file is selected.

 Deselect a File
To deselect a file, click outside the file list.

End Task

Task 15: Selecting Multiple Files That Are Next to Each Other

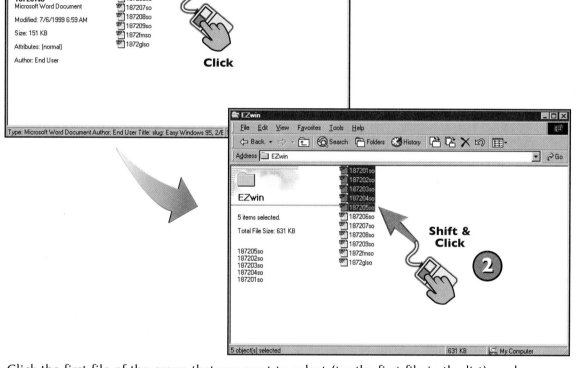

Click

Shift & Click

Windows Millennium enables you to easily select multiple files. If the files are listed together (next to each other in the listing), use this method to select them.

1 Click the first file of the group that you want to select (try the first file in the list), and then hold down the **Shift** key.

2 Click the last file in the group that you want to select (try the last file in the list); the first and last files, as well as all the files in between, are selected.

✓ **Select Folders**
You can select a group of folders using this same method.

✓ **Information Pane**
Check the information pane. It lists the number and size of the selected files.

Task 16: Selecting Multiple Files That Are Not Next to Each Other

Start Here

If the files you want to select are not grouped together, you can still select them using this method.

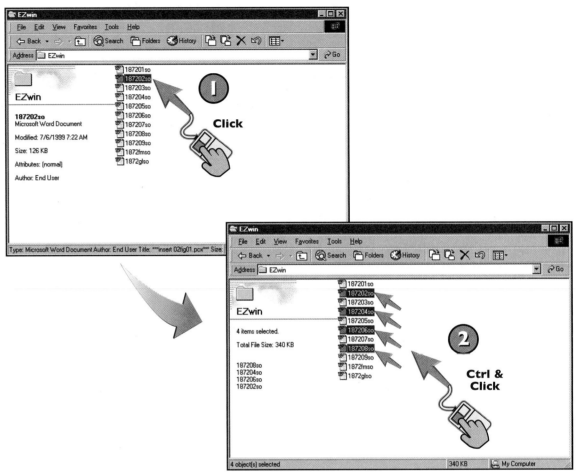

Click

Ctrl & Click

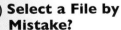 Click the first file that you want to select, and hold down the **Ctrl** key.

 While holding down the **Ctrl** key, click each file that you want to select. Each file you click remains selected.

Select a File by Mistake?
If you select a file by mistake, you can **Ctrl+Click** the file again to deselect it.

End Task

Task 17: Selecting All Files

For some tasks, such as making a backup copy of all files in a folder, you might want to select all files in a window. Windows Millennium provides a command for selecting all the files in a window.

Click

Selects all items in the window.

① Click the **Edit** menu, and then click the **Select All** command.

② All files are selected.

✔ **Change Selection**
To invert the selection (select unselected files and deselect selected files), use the **Edit, Invert Selection** command.

✔ **Keyboard Shortcut**
Press **Ctrl+A** to select all files.

Task 18: Copying a File to Another Folder

Windows makes it easy to copy files from one folder to another and from one disk to another. You might copy files to create a backup copy or to revise one copy while keeping the original file intact.

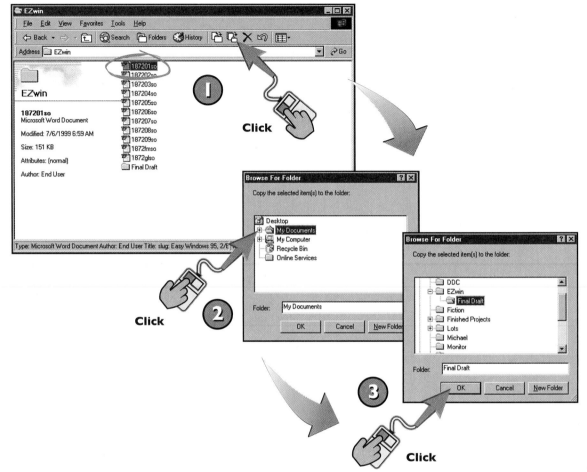

Click

Click

Click

✅ Drag-and-Drop Copying
To use drag-and-drop editing to copy files, display the **Folders** bar by clicking its button. Then in the pane on the right, display and select the files. Hold the **Ctrl** key and drag the file to its destination in the folder list on the left.

✅ Shortcuts
Alternatively, you can right-click the selected files and select **Copy** from the shortcut menu.

① Select the files you want to copy. Click the **Copy To** button.

② Display the folder into which you want to place the file. You can expand the folder listing by clicking the plus sign next to the icon, drive, or folder.

③ Click **OK**. Windows copies the files to the new location.

Task 19: Copying a File to a Floppy Disk

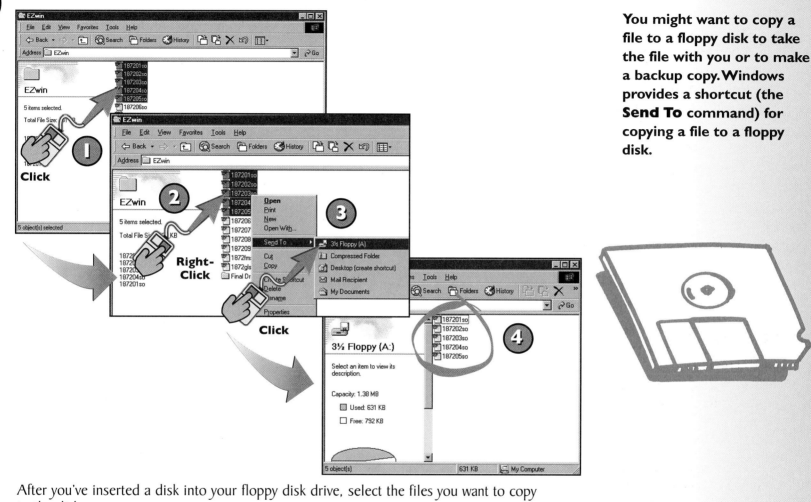

You might want to copy a file to a floppy disk to take the file with you or to make a backup copy. Windows provides a shortcut (the **Send To** command) for copying a file to a floppy disk.

(1) After you've inserted a disk into your floppy disk drive, select the files you want to copy to the disk.

(2) Right-click the selected files.

(3) Select the **Send To** command from the shortcut menu, and choose the appropriate floppy drive.

(4) The files are copied to that disk.

✅ **Disk Full?**
If the disk is full, you see an error message. Insert a different disk and click the **Retry** button.

Task 20: Moving a File

You might need to move files from one folder or drive to another (for example, to reorganize folders by putting similar files together in the same folder). You can also move a file that you accidentally saved in the wrong folder.

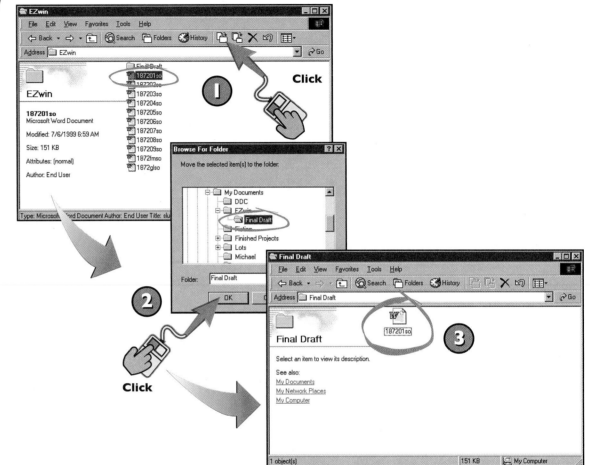

Click

Click

✅ **Undo Move**

If you make a mistake, you can undo the move by selecting the **Undo** command from the **Edit** menu.

✅ **Drag to Move**

You can also drag a file to a different folder. Display the **Folders** bar by clicking its button. Then in the right pane select the files you want to move. If you are moving from one folder to another, simply drag the files from that window to the drive or folder in the folders list on the left. If you are moving from one drive to another, hold down the **Shift** key and drag.

① Select the files you want to move, and click the **Move To** button.

② Display the folder in which you want to place the file, and click **OK**. You can expand the folder listing by clicking the plus sign next to the icon, drive, or folder.

③ Windows moves the files to the new location.

Task 21: Deleting a File

Start Here

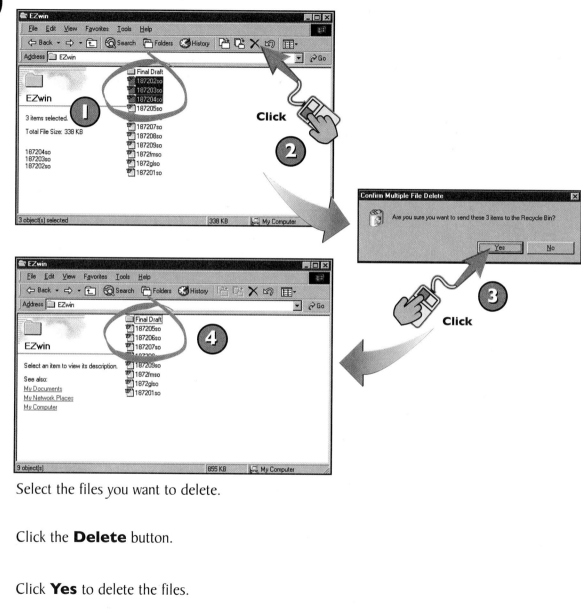

Click

Click

Confirm Multiple File Delete

Are you sure you want to send these 3 items to the Recycle Bin?

Yes   No

Eventually, your computer will become full of files, and you'll have a hard time organizing and storing them all. You can copy necessary files to floppy disks, tapes, and so on, and then delete the files from your hard drive to make room for new files. In addition, you will sometimes want to delete files you no longer need.

✓ **Undo the Deletion**
You can undo a deletion by selecting the **Undo** command from the **Edit** menu. Alternatively, you can retrieve the deleted item from the Recycle Bin, as covered in the next task.

✓ **Delete Shortcuts**
Other alternatives for deleting files and folders include right-clicking the folder or file and choosing **Delete** from the shortcut menu, and selecting the file or folder and pressing the **Delete** key on your keyboard.

① Select the files you want to delete.

② Click the **Delete** button.

③ Click **Yes** to delete the files.

④ Windows removes the files, placing them in the Recycle Bin.

Task 22: Undeleting a File or Folder

Sometimes you will delete a file or folder by mistake. You can retrieve the file or folder from the Recycle Bin (as long as the Recycle Bin has not been emptied) and return it to its original location.

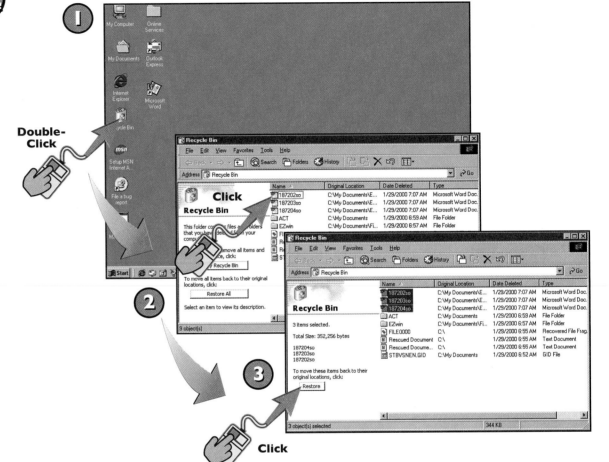

Double-Click

Click

 Clean Out the Recycle Bin
If you want to be permanently rid of the files in the Recycle Bin, you can empty it. Double-click the **Recycle Bin** icon and make sure that it doesn't contain anything you need to save. Then click the **Empty Recycle Bin** button. Windows displays the **Confirm Multiple File Delete** dialog box; click **Yes** to empty the Recycle Bin.

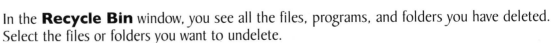

Click

1 Double-click the **Recycle Bin** icon on your desktop.

2 In the **Recycle Bin** window, you see all the files, programs, and folders you have deleted. Select the files or folders you want to undelete.

3 Click the **Restore** button. The files or folders are moved from the Recycle Bin to their original locations.

 End Task

Task 23: Finding Files and Folders

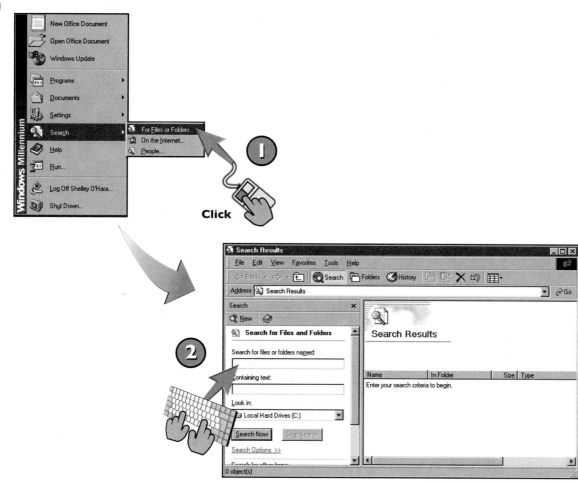

Click

After you've worked for months with your applications, your computer will become filled with various folders and files, which can make it nearly impossible for you to know where everything is. Luckily, Windows includes a command that helps you locate specific files or folders by name, file type, location, and so on.

Click **Start**, **Search**, **For Files or Folders**.

Type the name of the file you want to search for.

Task 23: Finding Files and Folders continued

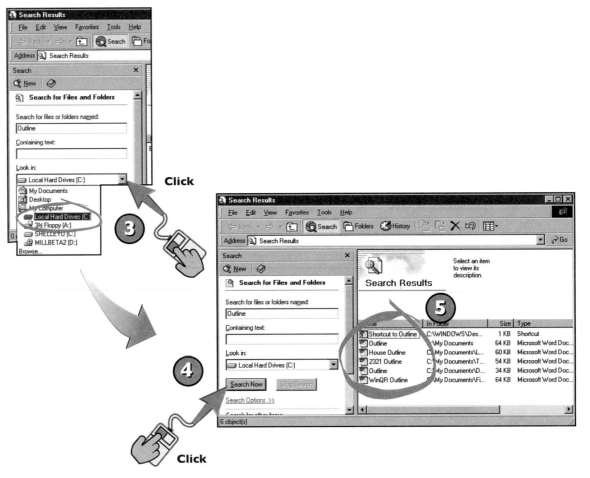

Click

Click

✅ **Search for Content**
If you do not know the name of the file but you know what it contains, type a unique word or phrase in the **Containing text** text box. Then search.

✅ **More Options**
For more options, click the **Search Options** link in the **Search Results** dialog box.

3 To change the drive on which Windows will conduct the search, display the **Look in** list box and choose the drives from the drop-down list.

4 Click the **Search Now** button.

5 Windows searches the selected drive and displays a list of found files in the right pane of the window. You can double-click any of the listed files or folders to go to that file or folder.

End Task

Task 24: Creating a Shortcut to a File or Folder

Start Here

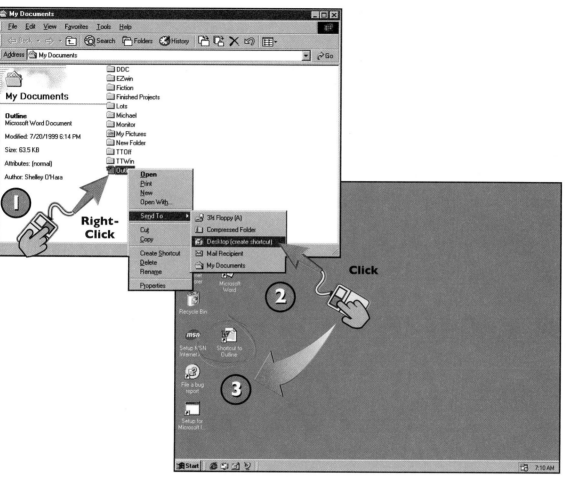

Right-Click

Click

If you often use the same file or folder, you might want fast access to it. If so, you can create a shortcut icon for the file or folder on the desktop. Double-clicking a file's shortcut icon opens the file in the program you used to create the file. Double-clicking a folder displays the contents of the folder in a window.

① Open the folder or drive containing the file for which you want to create a shortcut icon, and right-click its icon.

② Select **Send To**, **Desktop (create shortcut)**.

③ Windows adds the shortcut icon to your desktop. (You can close the other windows to better see the shortcut icon, as I've done here.)

✓ **Rename a Shortcut**
To rename the shortcut icon, right-click it and choose **Rename.** Type a new name and press **Enter.**

✓ **Delete a Shortcut**
To delete the shortcut icon, right-click it and choose **Delete** or drag the icon to the Recycle Bin.

Using Applications in Windows Millennium

One advantage to using Windows Millennium is the enormous number of available Windows applications. You can use many word-processing, database, spreadsheet, drawing, and other programs in Windows. This variety of applications provides all the tools you need to perform your everyday tasks.

Windows applications are easy to open and use, and enable you to create documents. Two important tasks are saving your work and opening your saved work, both covered here. You'll also learn some skills that work for many applications, including copying and moving text.

Tasks

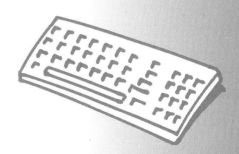

Task 1: Starting an Application from a Shortcut Icon

In addition to the **Start** menu, you can also start programs from shortcut icons. Some programs automatically create shortcut icons, placing them on the desktop. You can also add shortcut icons to programs yourself (covered in Part 10, "Setting Up Programs"). This task covers how to start an application from a shortcut icon.

Start Here

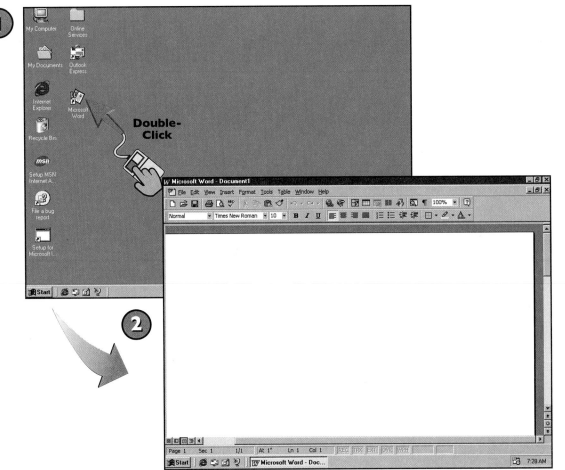

Double-Click

✓ The Start Menu
To use the **Start** menu, see Part 1, Task 14, "Starting an Application from the Start Menu," for instructions on starting a program from this menu.

⚠ WARNING!
If nothing happens when you double-click the icon, or if the icon moves, it might be because you haven't clicked quickly enough or because you clicked and dragged by accident. Be sure to press the mouse button twice quickly.

① Double-click the shortcut icon on the desktop.

② The application starts and displays in its own window (Word, in this example).

End Task

Task 2: Starting an Application and Opening a Document

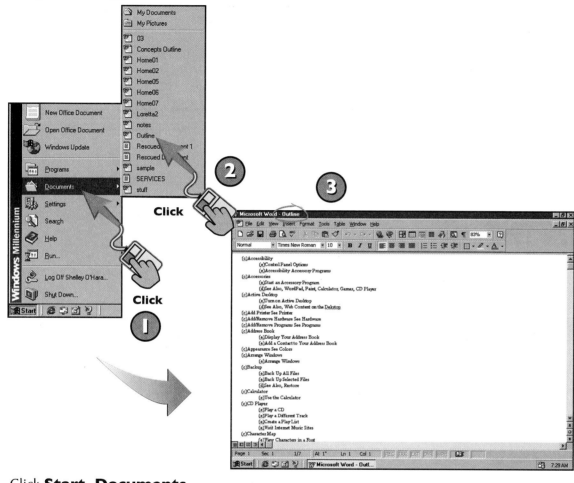

Click

Click

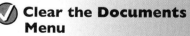

If you want to work on a document that you recently had open (in Word, for example), you can use a shortcut to both start Word and open the document. Windows Millennium's **Documents** menu lists the 15 documents that you have opened most recently.

① Click **Start**, **Documents**.

② Click the document you want to work on.

③ The program for that document starts and the document opens.

✓ Clear the Documents Menu
To clear the **Documents** menu, click the **Start** menu, choose **Settings**, and then choose **Taskbar and Start Menu**. Click the **Advanced** tab, and click the **Clear** button.

Task 3: Starting an Application from a File Icon

Sometimes you might be browsing the contents of your system and see a file you want to open. You don't have to start that program and then open the document. Instead, you can start the program and open the document using the file icon.

Start Here

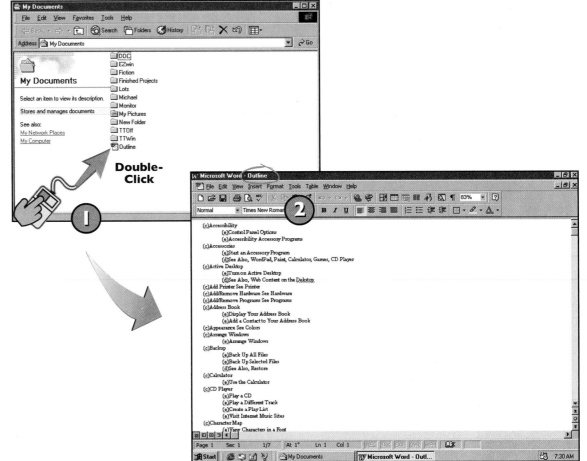

Double-Click

 Browse for Files
You can browse for files using the **My Computer** or **My Documents** icons. For more information on displaying files, see Part 2, "Working with Disks, Folders, and Files."

Page
62

1 Display and double-click the file you want to open.

2 The program for that document starts and the document opens.

End Task

Task 4: Switching Between Applications

Start Here

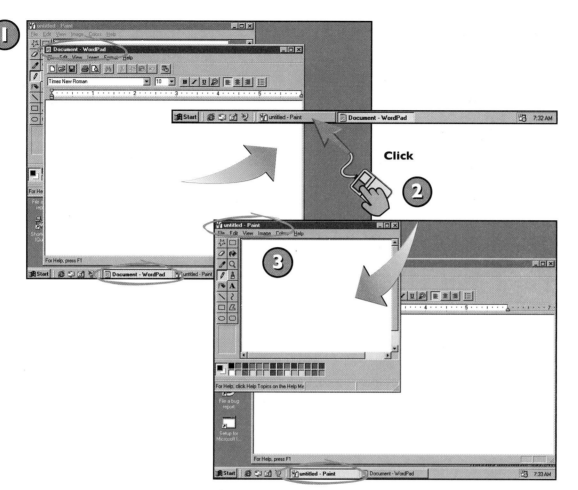

Click

Because you most likely work with more than one type of document at the same time, you need a way to switch from one program to another. For example, you might want to compare price figures from an Excel worksheet with a price list you've set up in Word. You might want to copy text from a WordPad document to a Paint picture. Switching between applications enables you not only to compare data, but also to share data.

✔ **Close an Application**
To close an application, use the **File, Exit** command or click the **Close (X)** button for the program window.

✔ **How Many?**
The number of programs you can have open at any one time depends on the amount of RAM (random-access memory) in your system.

① After you've started two programs, look at the taskbar. You should see a button for each program. In this case, the **WordPad** button is selected, so WordPad is displayed onscreen.

② Click the button for the program you want to switch to (in this case, **Paint**).

③ That program becomes the active program.

End Task

Task 5: Saving a Document

You save documents and files so that you can refer to them later for printing, editing, copying, and so on. The first time you save a file, you must assign that file a name and folder (or location). You save documents pretty much the same way in all Windows applications; this task shows you how to save a document in WordPad.

Start Here

Click

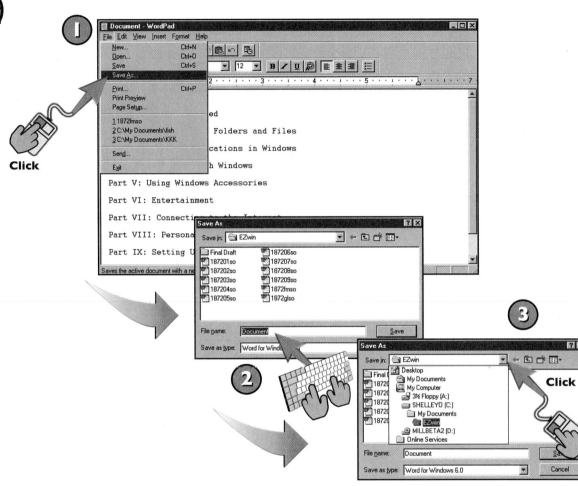

✓ **Save Again**
After you've saved and named a file, you can simply click **File** and select **Save** to resave that file to the same location with the same name. Any changes you have made since the last save are reflected in the file.

✓ **Save with New Name**
To save the file with a different name or in a different location, use the **Save As** command and enter a different filename or folder.

Click **File**, **Save As** in your open application.

The program might propose a name for the file. You can either accept this name or type a new name.

To save the document in another drive, click the **Save in** drop-down list and select the drive you want.

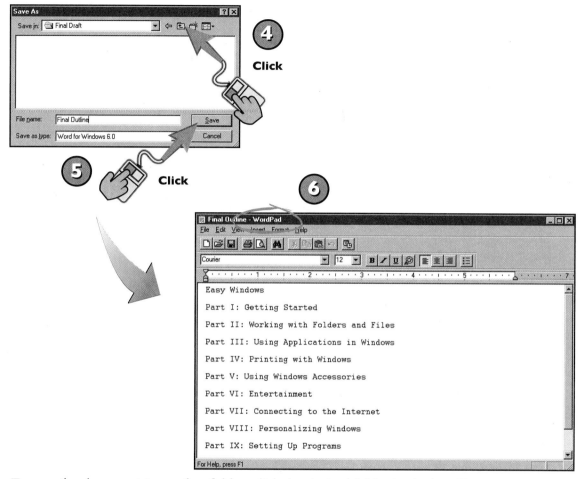

4 To save the document in another folder, click the desired folder in the list. To move up through the folder structure, click the **Up One Level** button.

5 Click the **Save** button.

6 The application saves the file and returns to the document window. The document name is listed in the title bar.

Task 6: Opening a Document

When you save a document, the program records the document information as a file. And the purpose of saving a document is to make it available for later use. You can open any of the documents you have saved. You can then make changes or print the document.

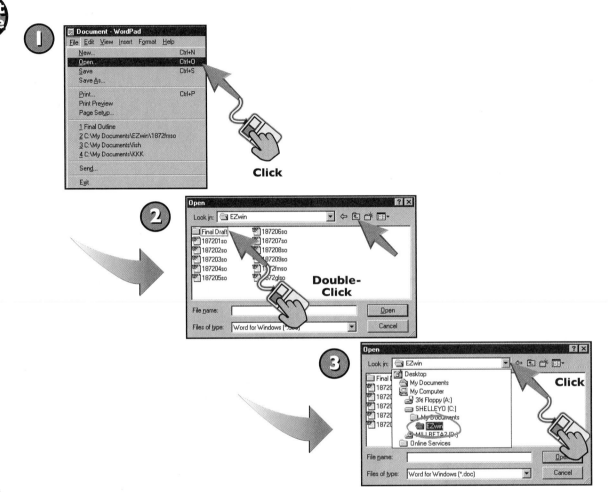

Click

Double-Click

Click

(1) Click **File**, and then click the **Open** command.

(2) Navigate to and double-click the folder that contains the file. You can use the **Up One Level** button to move up through the folders. (If the file is listed, skip to step 4.)

(3) If the file is on another drive, display the **Look in** drop-down list and select the drive where you placed the file.

Next Step

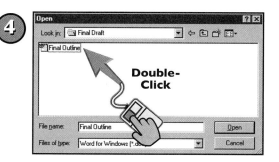

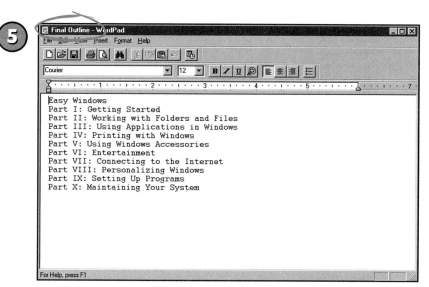

④ When you find the file you seek, double-click it.

⑤ The file is opened.

✅ **Shortcut**
As a shortcut, click **File**. Notice that the last files opened are listed near the bottom of the menu. You can open any of these files by clicking them in the **File** menu.

Task 7: Switching Between Open Documents

Start Here

In most programs, you can work with several documents at once. The number of documents you can have open depends on your system memory and the program. Simply click **File** and select the **Open** command to open the files you want to work with. Then you can easily switch between any of the open documents.

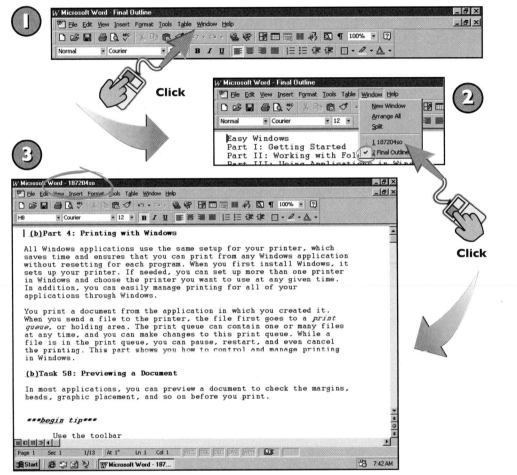

Click

Click

✓ **Switching Documents Versus Applications**
Don't confuse switching between documents with switching between applications. For more information, refer to Task 4, "Switching Between Applications."

✓ **No Window Menu?**
If the program does not have a **Window** menu, you probably cannot work in multiple documents. For example, in WordPad, you cannot have more than one document open at a time.

① Click **Window**.

② Notice that the current document has a check mark next to its name. Click the document that you want to switch to.

③ The document you just clicked in the **Window** menu becomes the active document.

End Task

Task 8: Creating a New Document

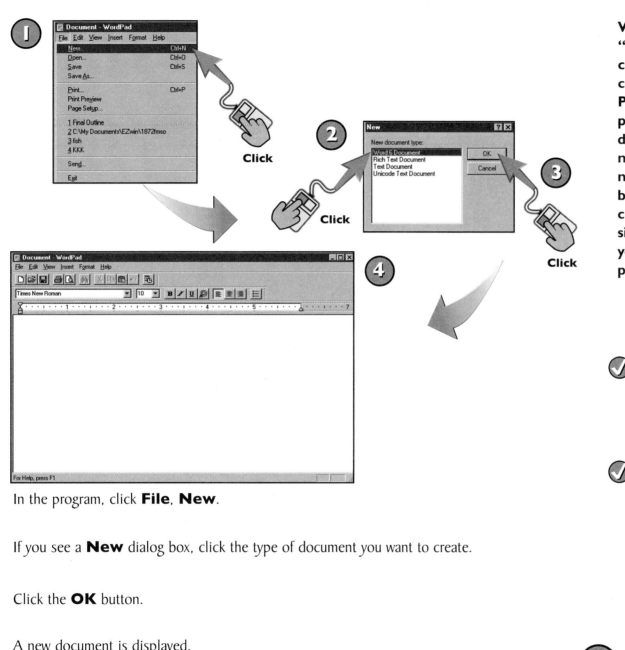

Click

Click

Click

When you want a new "sheet" of paper, you can create a new document. For complex programs such as **PowerPoint** (a presentation program) and **Access** (a database program), you might be prompted to make some selections before the new document is created. For others, you simply select the template you want. (A *template* is a predesigned document.)

✓ **Shortcut**
As a shortcut, you can click the **New** button to create a new document based on the default template.

✓ **Exit the Program**
If you click the **Close** button on the program window, you exit the program. Be sure to use the **Close** button for the document window if you want to remain in the program but close the document.

1. In the program, click **File**, **New**.

2. If you see a **New** dialog box, click the type of document you want to create.

3. Click the **OK** button.

4. A new document is displayed.

Task 9: Closing a Document

When you save a docu-
ment, it remains open so
that you can continue
working. If you want to
close the document, you
can easily do so. You should
close documents that you
are no longer using in order
to free up memory.

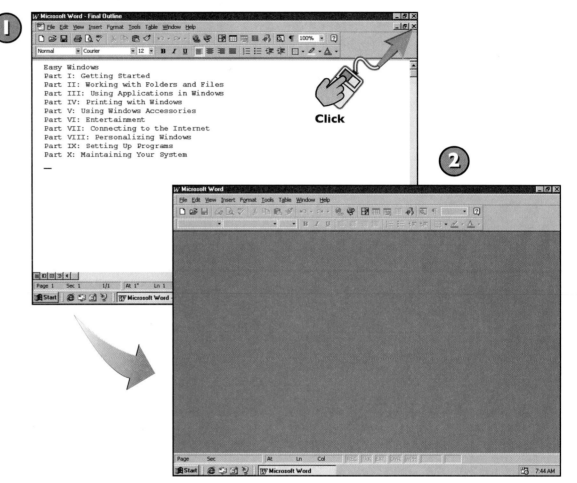

Click

Use the File Menu
You can also use the **File**
menu to close a document.
Click **File**, and then choose
Close. If you have not
saved your document, you
will be prompted to do so.

Click the **Close** button.

The document is closed but the program remains open. You can create a new document or
open an existing document.

Task 10: Selecting Text

Start Here

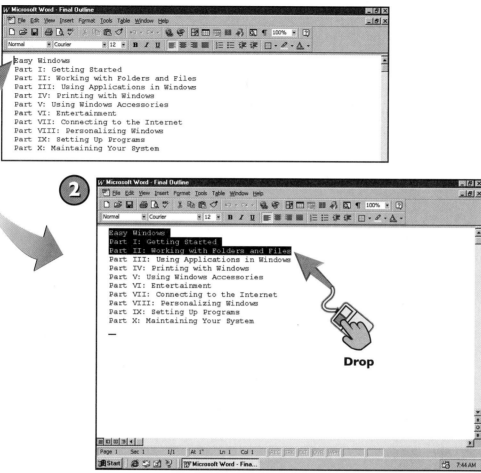

Click & Drag

Drop

Knowing how to select data (text, images, and so on) is one of any program's key tasks. For example, you can select text and then delete it, move it, copy it, change its appearance, and more.

① Click at the beginning of the text you want to select.

② Hold down the mouse button and drag across the text, then release the mouse button. The selected text appears highlighted.

✓ **Select an Image**
To select an image, click it once.

✓ **Use the Keyboard**
If you prefer to use the keyboard to select text, hold down the **Shift** key and use the arrow keys to highlight the text you want to select.

✓ **Deselect Text**
To deselect text, click outside the text.

Task 11: Copying Text

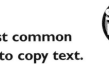

One of the most common editing tasks is to copy text. You can copy text and paste the copy into the current document or into another document.

Copy to Another Document

To copy data from one open document to another, select the text and then move to the document where you want to paste the text using the **Window** menu.

Select the text you want to copy.

Click **Edit**, and then select the **Copy** command.

Click the spot in the document where you want to put the copied data.

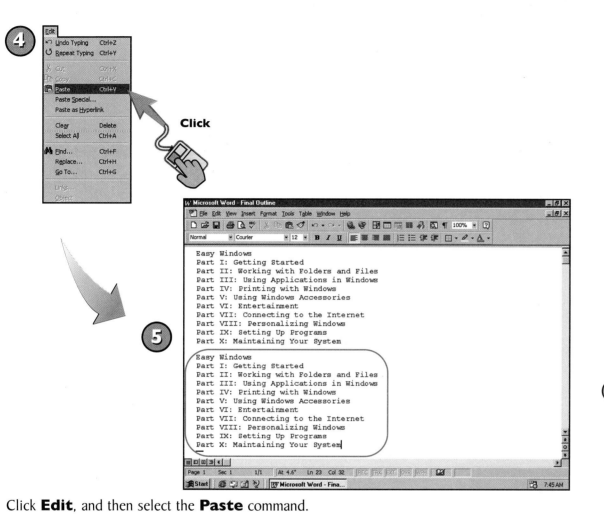

Click

 Click **Edit**, and then select the **Paste** command.

The data is pasted into the document.

Can't Paste?
If the **Paste** command is grayed out, it means you have not copied anything. Be sure to click **Edit** and then select the **Copy** command before you try to paste the text.

Shortcuts
Most programs include toolbar buttons and keyboard shortcuts for **Cut**, **Copy**, and **Paste**. You can also use these.

Task 12: Moving Text

Just as you can copy text, you can move text from one location in a document to another location in the same document. You can also move text from one document to another. Moving text is similar to copying text, except that when you move something it is deleted from its original location.

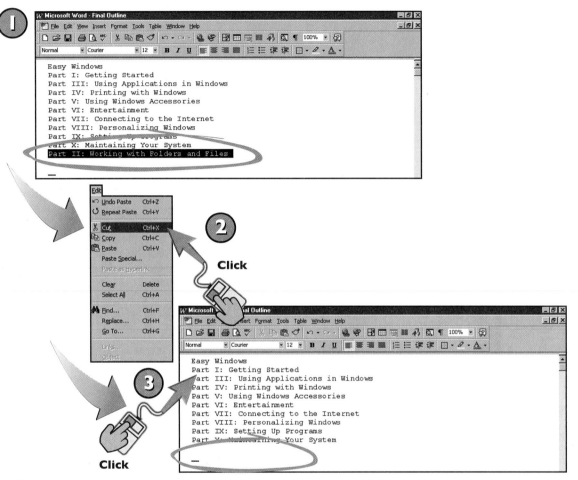

Start Here

Click

Click

✓ **Move to Another Application**
For help on moving data from one application to another, see Task 14, "Moving Data Between Applications."

(1) Select the text you want to move.

(2) Click **Edit**, and then click the **Cut** command. Windows deletes the data from the document and places it in the *Clipboard,* a hidden temporary holding spot.

(3) Click in the document where you want to place the text.

Next Step

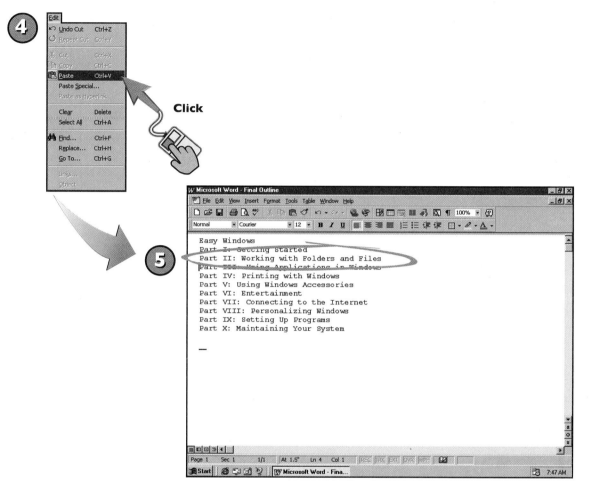

Click

Click **Edit**, and then select the **Paste** command.

The text is pasted into the new location.

 Undo a Move
You can undo a paste operation if you change your mind after performing the action. Simply click **Edit**, and then select the **Undo Paste** command to remove the text you just pasted.

 Shortcuts
You can also use the keyboard shortcut **Ctrl+X** to cut, and use the keyboard command **Ctrl+V** to paste. Look also for toolbar buttons for **Cut**, **Copy**, and **Paste**.

End Task

Task 13: Copying Data Between Applications

You can copy data from a document in one application and paste it into another document in another application to save time typing. In addition to being able to copy text, you can copy spreadsheets, figures, charts, clip art, and so on. Using copied text and graphics saves you time in your work.

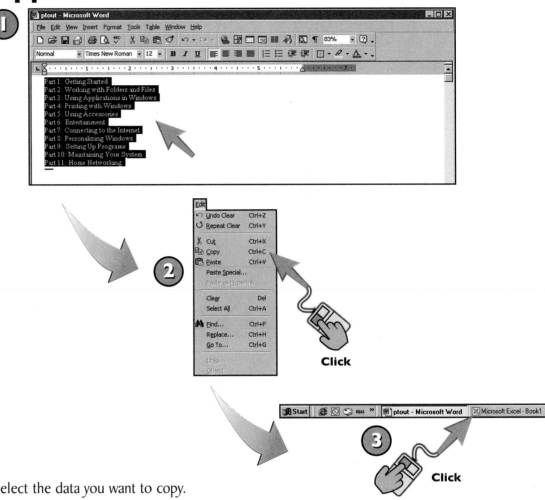

1. Select the data you want to copy.

2. Click **Edit**, and then click the **Copy** command.

3. Click the taskbar button representing the program you want to switch to (in this case, **Microsoft Excel**). If the program isn't started, start the program.

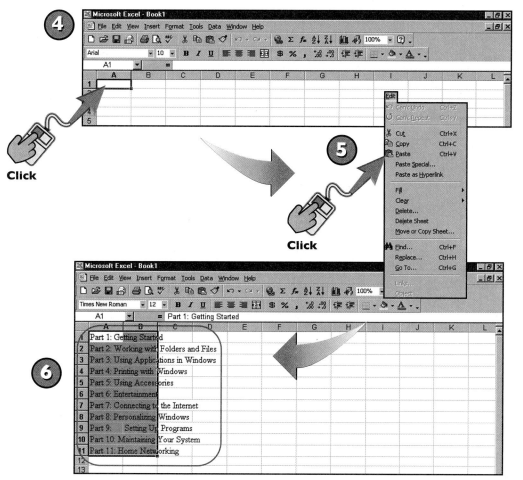

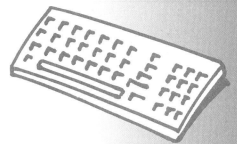

Click

Click

In the document, click the location where you want to paste the copied data.

Click **Edit**, and then click the **Paste** command.

The data is pasted into the document.

✅ **Use a Shortcut**
You can also select the text and right-click the selection to display a shortcut menu. Select **Copy** from this menu. Right-click where you want to paste the text, and then select **Paste**.

You can also move information from one application to another. For example, you can cut a table of numerical data from Word and paste it into a report in Excel.

Task 14: Moving Data Between Applications

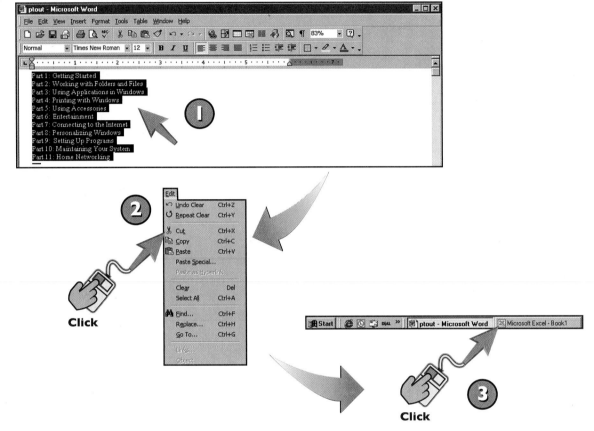

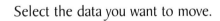

① Select the data you want to move.

② Click **Edit**, and then click the **Cut** command. Windows deletes the data from the document and places it in the *Clipboard,* a temporary holding spot.

③ Click the taskbar button representing the program you want to switch to (in this case, **Microsoft Excel**).

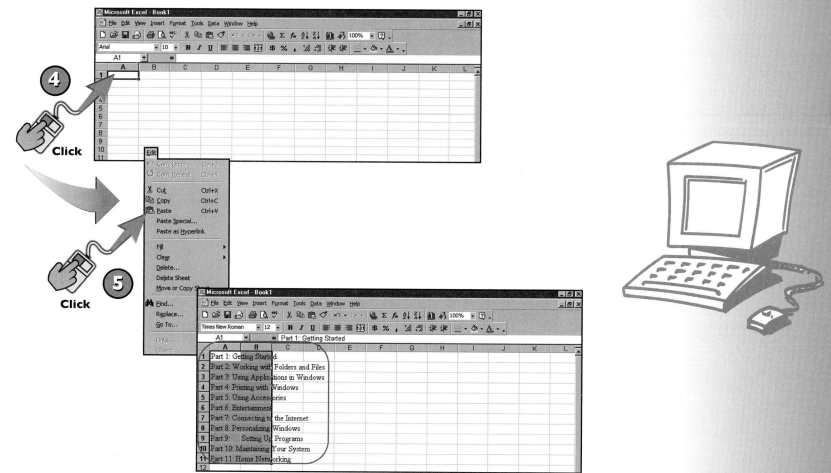

 **4** Click in the spreadsheet where you want to place the data.

5 Click **Edit**, and then click the **Paste** command.

6 The data is pasted into the spreadsheet.

 Undo a Move
Use the **Undo** command
to undo the move.

You might link data between applications if you want the data to be updated automatically when you edit or add to the source document. Linking data saves you time because you must edit the information only once; Windows then updates any linked files for you.

Task 15: Linking Data Between Applications

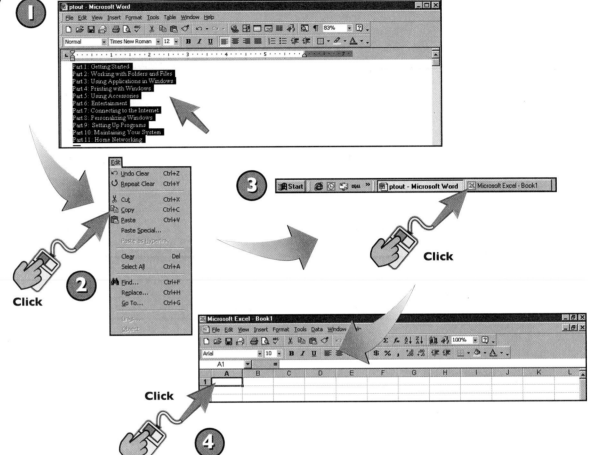

1 In the source document, select the data you want to link.

2 Click **Edit**, and then click the **Copy** command.

3 Click the taskbar button representing the program and document where you want to paste the linked data.

4 Click in the document where you want the linked data to go.

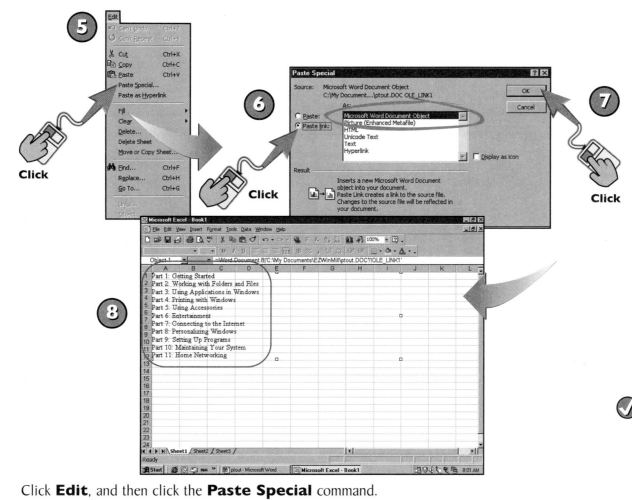

Click (step 5)

Click (step 6)

Click (step 7)

5. Click **Edit**, and then click the **Paste Special** command.

6. Select the **Paste Link** radio button, and then select the format you want to paste from the **As** list box.

7. Click the **OK** button.

8. Windows inserts the data with a link between the destination and the source files.

Update Links
Check the program documentation for commands on updating and maintaining links.

Formats
The available formats in the **As** list box depend on the type of data you're pasting and control how the data is inserted into the document.

End
Task

Printing with Windows

All Windows applications use the same setup for your printer, which saves time and ensures that you can print from any Windows application without resetting for each program. When you first install Windows, it sets up your printer. If needed, you can set up more than one printer in Windows and choose the printer you want to use at any given time. In addition, you can easily manage printing for all your applications through Windows.

You print a document from the application in which you created it. When you send a file to the printer, the file first goes to a *print queue*, or holding area. The print queue can contain one or many files at any time, and you can make changes to this print queue. While a file is in the print queue, you can pause, restart, and even cancel the printing. This part shows you how to control and manage printing in Windows.

Tasks

Task 1: Previewing a Document

In most applications, you can preview a document to check the margins, heads, graphics placement, and so on before you print.

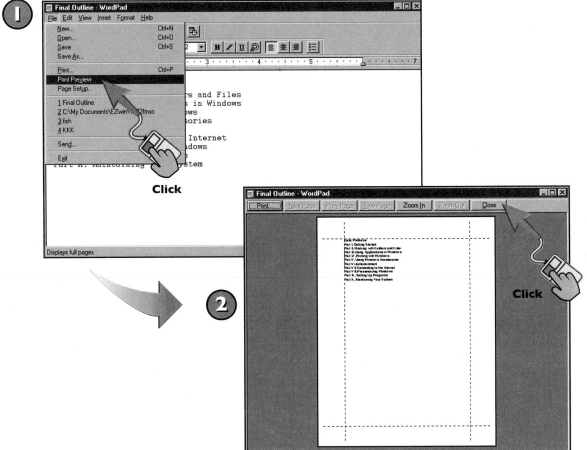

Click

Click

✅ **Toolbar**
The **Print Preview** view usually includes a toolbar for working with the document. Using buttons in this toolbar, you can magnify the view, print, change the margins, and more.

✅ **No Preview?**
Most programs have a preview option, but if you don't see this command listed in your program, it might not be available. You will have to print the document to see how it looks.

Click **File** and select the **Print Preview** command.

You see a preview of the current document. After you finish viewing the preview, click the **Close** button.

Task 2: Printing a Document

Start Here

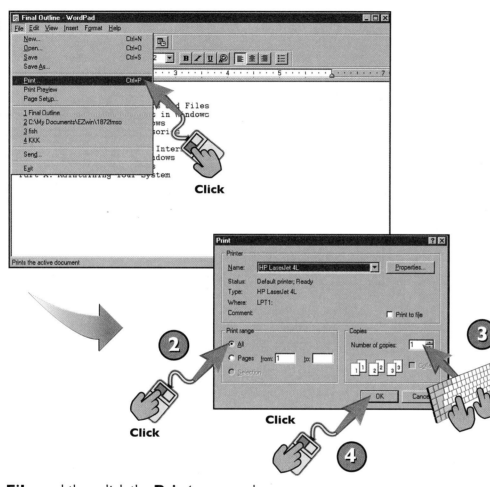

Click

Click

Click

When you first install Windows, it sets up a primary printer, allowing you to print from any application using this printer. Printing your documents gives you a paper copy you can proofread, use in reports, give to co-workers, and so on.

① Click **File**, and then click the **Print** command.

② In the **Print** dialog, specify a page range.

③ Enter the number of copies you want printed.

④ Click the **OK** button.

 Shortcut
As a shortcut, use the **Print** button in your toolbar. Alternatively, you can use a keyboard shortcut (usually **Ctrl+P**) to print.

Use Another Printer
If you want to use a printer other than the default, choose the printer you want to use from the **Name** drop-down list in the **Print** dialog box.

End Task

Task 3: Viewing the Print Queue

The print queue lists the documents that have been sent to a printer, and it shows how far along the printing is. Using the print queue, you can pause, restart, or cancel print jobs. This task shows how to view the print queue.

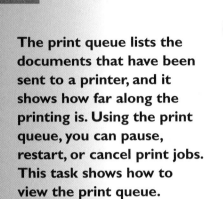

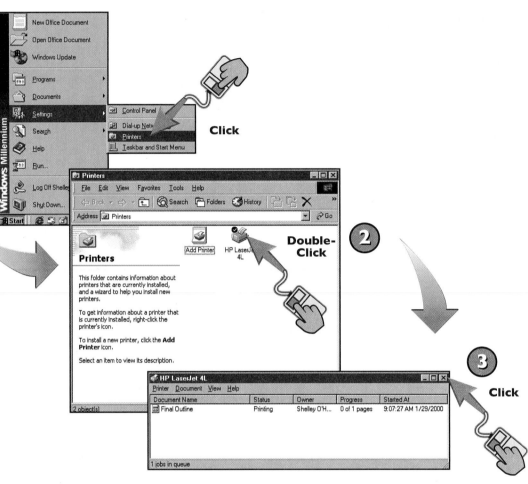

Start Here

Click

Double-Click

Click

(✓) **Double-Click the Icon**
You can display the print queue by double-clicking the **Printer** icon in the taskbar (on the left side). This icon appears whenever you are printing something.

(✓) **Empty?**
If the print queue window is empty, either the print job never made it to the queue or it was already processed by the printer.

1 Click the **Start** button, click the **Settings** command, and then choose **Printers**.

2 Double-click the printer whose print queue you want to view.

3 The printer window displays a list of the documents in the queue as well as statistics about the documents being printed. Click the **Close** button to close the queue.

End Task

Task 4: Pausing and Restarting the Printer

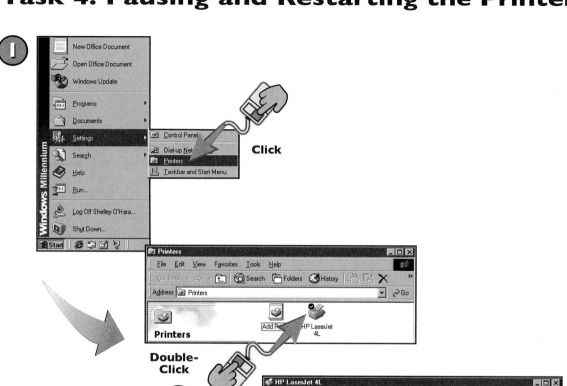

You might want to pause printing when you must make a change in the text or when you want to load a different paper type. You can easily stop the printing from the **Printers** folder, and you can restart it at any time.

✔️ Nothing Listed?
You must be quick to pause or stop a short print job. If nothing appears in the print queue, it probably means that the entire print job has already been sent to the printer.

✔️ Pause a Job
You can use the **Document** menu in the print queue to pause printing on a specific job Select the job you want to pause, and choose the **Pause Printing** command from the **Document** menu.

Click the **Start** button, click the **Settings** command, and then choose **Printers**.

Double-click the printer whose print queue you want to view.

Click **Printer**, and then select the **Pause Printing** command.

✔️ Restart the Printer
To restart the printer after you have paused it, click **Printer**, and then click the **Pause Printing** command again.

Task 5: Canceling Printing

If you discover an error in the job you are printing, or if you decide that you need to add something to it, you can cancel the print job. Canceling the print job prevents you from wasting time and paper.

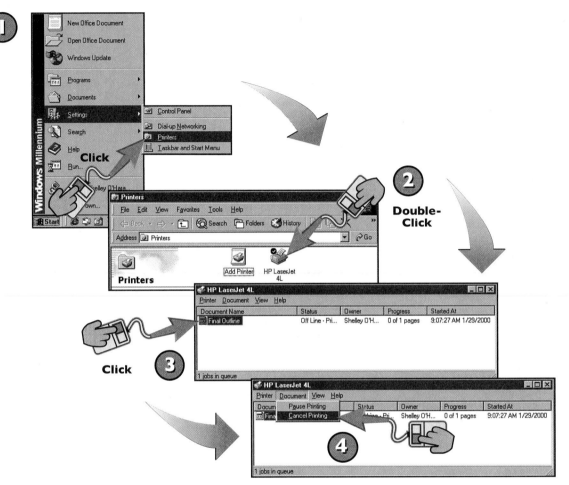

Nothing Listed?
Depending on your computer and your printer, the print job might be listed in the print queue for only a few seconds before it is sent to the printer. You might not be able to cancel it.

1 Click the **Start**, **Settings**, and then click **Printers**.

2 Double-click the printer whose print queue you want to view.

3 In the print queue, click the print job you want to cancel.

4 Click **Document**, and then select the **Cancel Printing** command.

End Task

Task 6: Setting the Default Printer

Start Here

1

New Office Document
Open Office Document
Windows Update
Programs
Documents
Settings   →   Control Panel
Search   →   Dial-up Networking
Click   Help   Printers
Run...   Taskbar and Start Menu

elley O'Hara...
own...

Start

If you have more than one printer connected, you must select one as the default. The default printer you set in Windows is the printer your applications automatically use when you choose to print. The default printer is the one on which you want most of your documents printed.

3

Printers

File   Edit   View   Favorites   Tools   Help

Open
Pause Printing
✓ Set as Default   Search   Folders   History

Purge Print Documents

Capture Printer Port...   Add Printer   HP LaserJet
End Capture...   4L

Create Shortcut
Delete
Rename
Properties

Close

Click

2

Click

Specifies that the selected printer is the default printer.

1 Click the **Start** button, **Settings**, and then click the **Printers** command.

2 Select the printer you want to choose as the default.

3 Click **File**, and then click the **Set as Default** command.

Change the Default
To use a different printer, follow this same procedure but select the new printer you want to use as the default.

Task 7: Changing Printer Settings

You can easily change printer settings. You might, for example, switch to a new, updated printer driver (a *driver* is a file that enables Windows to use your printer). Alternatively, you might change the port to which your printer connects to make room for another external device, such as a modem or tape drive.

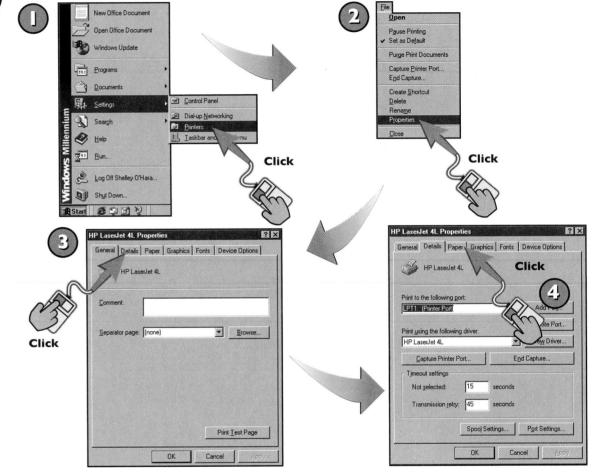

✓ Port Selection

Use the drop-down list to select from common ports. A *port* is a connection on the back of your computer, in which you can use a cable to connect the computer to a printer (or other device).

✓ What's a Timeout?

Timeout settings specify how long Windows will wait before reporting an error to you.

1 Click the **Start** button, **Settings**, and then choose **Printers**.

2 After you select the printer you want to modify, click **File**, and then select the **Properties** command.

3 Click the **Details** tab.

4 Make the necessary changes to the printer port, driver, timeout settings, and so on. After you finish, click the **Paper** tab.

Next Step

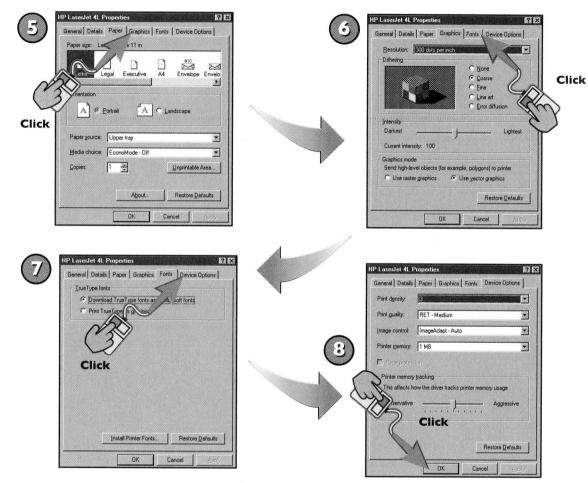

Page
91

Change for One Job
Changing the printer's properties changes them for all documents you print on this printer. If you want to change properties for just one document, use the **Page Settings or Print Setup** command in the particular program you are using to print.

Restore Defaults
If you make a change in the **Paper, Graphics, Fonts,** or **Device Options** tab and change your mind about the changes, you can choose the **Restore Defaults** button in that tab to cancel just that tab's changes.

Not Sure About an Option?
Some of these options are pretty obscure. If you need help on an option, right-click it and select **What's This?** to see a pop-up explanation.

5️⃣ Make changes to the paper size, orientation, source, number of copies, and other options. After you finish, click the **Graphics** tab.

6️⃣ Make changes to the print resolution, dithering, shading intensity, and graphics mode. After you finish, click the **Fonts** tab.

7️⃣ Install printer fonts or new font cartridges. Choose any font cartridge you have added to enable the use of its fonts in Windows. After you finish, click the **Device Options** tab.

8️⃣ Use the **Device Options** tab to choose printed text quality; the available options depend on your printer. After you finish, click the **OK** button.

Task 8: Adding a Printer

You can add a new printer to your Windows setup using a step-by-step guide called a *wizard* that Windows provides. Use the wizard any time you get a new printer or change printers.

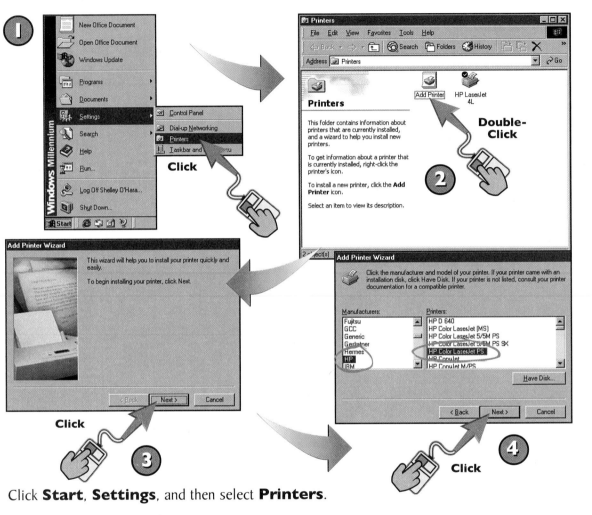

Start Here

Click

Double-Click

Click

Click

✔ Use Disk

If you want to use drivers supplied by your printer manufacturer, click the **Have Disk** button instead of clicking **Next**. Insert the appropriate disk and follow the onscreen instructions.

1 Click **Start**, **Settings**, and then select **Printers**.

2 Double-click the **Add Printer** icon.

3 Click the **Next** button to continue with the installation.

4 Select the name of your printer's manufacturer from the **Manufacturers** list box, select the appropriate printer from the **Printers** list box, and then click **Next**.

Next Step

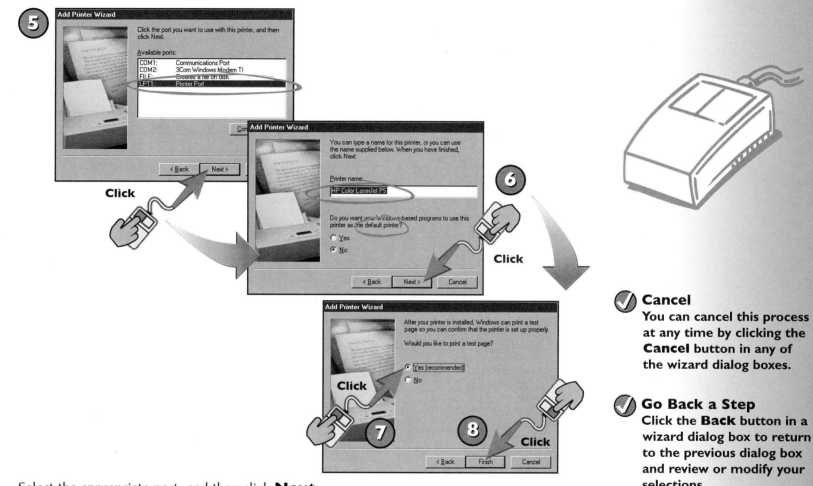

Click

Click

Click

Click

(5) Select the appropriate port, and then click **Next**.

(6) Enter a name for the printer or accept the one Windows has given it, and then select whether you want the new printer to be the default printer. After you finish, click **Next**.

(7) Click the **Yes** radio button to print a test page.

(8) Click the **Finish** button. Windows adds the new printer's icon to the **Printers** folder.

Task 9: Deleting a Printer

If you get a new printer, you can delete the setup for the old printer so that you don't get confused about which printer is which. Deleting a printer removes it from the available list of printers.

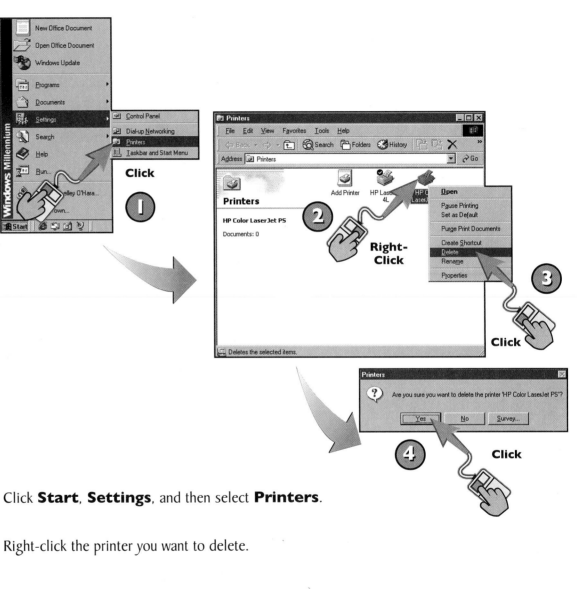

Start Here

Click

Right-Click

Click

Click

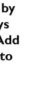

✓ Undo a Deletion
If you delete a printer by mistake, you can always add it back using the Add Printer Wizard (refer to Task 8, "Adding a Printer").

① Click **Start**, **Settings**, and then select **Printers**.

② Right-click the printer you want to delete.

③ Select the **Delete** command from the shortcut menu.

④ Click the **Yes** button to confirm the deletion.

End Task

Task 10: Adding a Printer Icon to the Desktop

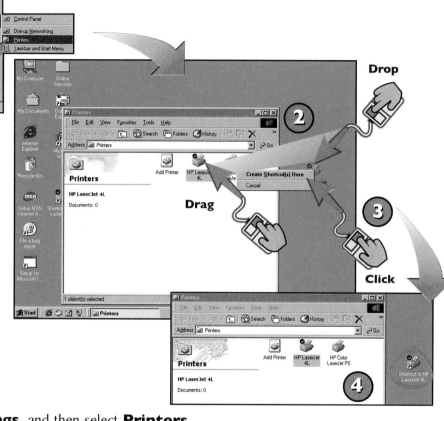

Start Here

For fast access to your printer, you can add a printer icon to your desktop. You can then double-click this icon to view the print queue. You can also drag documents from a file window to the printer icon to print the documents.

Drop

Drag

Click

① Click **Start**, **Settings**, and then select **Printers**.

② Drag the icon from the printer window to the desktop using the right mouse button.

③ Select **Create Shortcut(s) Here** from the quick menu that appears when you release the mouse button.

④ The printer shortcut is added to your desktop.

✅ **Use the Right Mouse Button**
Be sure to drag with the right mouse button to create a shortcut icon.

✅ **Delete the Icon**
To delete the shortcut icon, right-click it, and then select **Delete** from the shortcut menu. When prompted to confirm the deletion, click the **Yes** button.

End Task

Task 11: Viewing Fonts

Windows can use two types of fonts: the fonts built in to your printer and the fonts installed on your system. The installed fonts are files that tell Windows how to print in that font. The fonts you can select to use in a document depend on the fonts installed on your system. You can view a list of fonts and see an example of any of the available fonts.

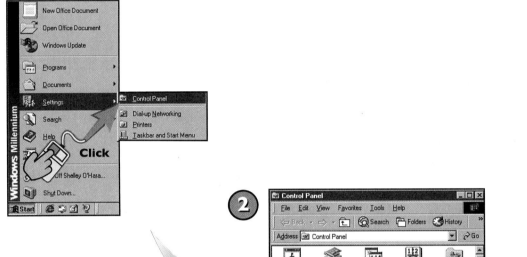

Click

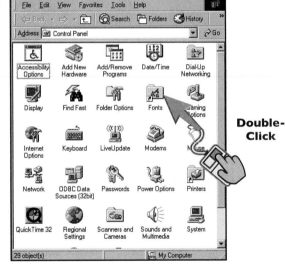

Double-Click

✔ View List

You can view the fonts by list rather than by icon. To do so, click the **List** button in the toolbar. Alternatively, open the **View** menu and select **List**. You can also view similar fonts by selecting **View, List Fonts by Similarity**.

① Click **Start**, **Settings**, and select **Control Panel**.

② Double-click the **Fonts** icon.

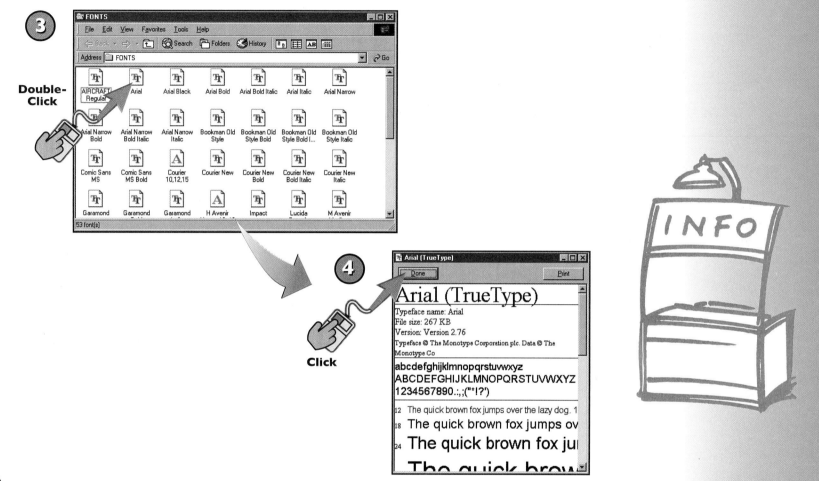

Double-Click

(3) You see the available fonts. To view a sample of the font, double-click the font name.

(4) Click the **Done** button.

Click

✓ **Print a Font**
To print a sample of the font, click the **Print** button in the **Font** dialog box.

End Task

Task 12: Adding Fonts

You can purchase additional fonts to add to your system. When you do so, you can install them in Windows so that you can use them with any Windows programs.

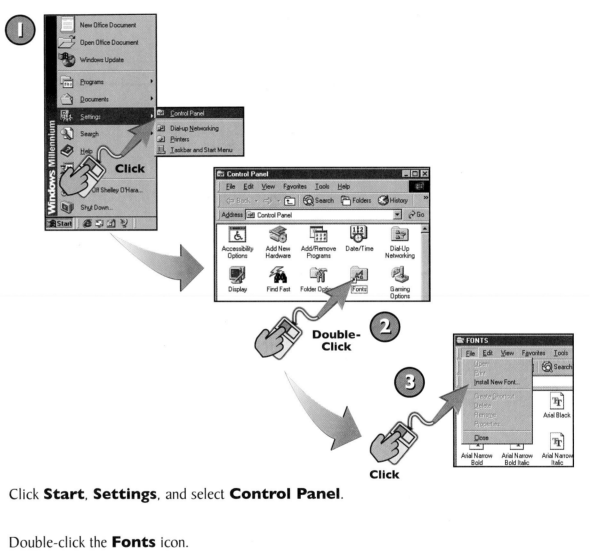

Click **Start**, **Settings**, and select **Control Panel**.

Double-click the **Fonts** icon.

Open the **File** menu and choose **Install New Font**.

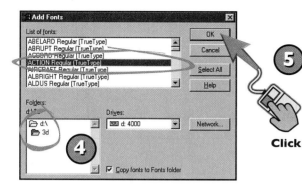

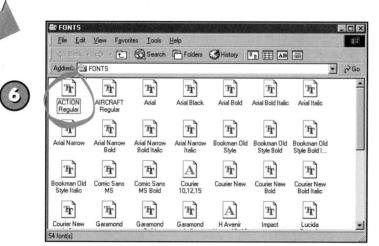

Select the drive and folder where the font is stored.

Select the font you want to install, and then click **OK**.

The font is installed.

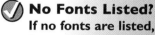
No Fonts Listed?
If no fonts are listed, it's
because no font files are in
the selected folder. Be sure
to select the drive and
folder where the files are
stored.

Select All Fonts
To select all the fonts, click
the **Select All** button.

Using Windows Accessories

Windows Millennium provides several accessories, or applications, that you can use to help you in your work. These accessories are not full-featured programs, but they are useful for specific jobs in the Windows environment. Accessories include a calculator, a painting program, a word processor, a text editor, and Internet applications. (The entertainment programs are covered in this part. Internet applications are discussed in Part 7, "Connecting to Online Services and the Internet.")

Tasks

Task 1: Using Calculator

If you need to perform a quick calculation, use the Calculator program included with Windows Millennium. You can add, subtract, multiply, divide, figure percentages, and more with this handy tool.

✓ **Scientific Calculator**
To use a more complex scientific calculator, click the calculator's **View** menu, and then click **Scientific**.

✓ **Copy Results to Document**
You can copy the results of a calculation into a document. To do so, select the results, click **Edit**, and then choose **Copy**. Then move to the document where you want to paste the results, click **Edit**, and then choose **Paste**.

✓ **Use the Keypad**
To use the numeric keypad to enter numbers, press the **Num Lock** button. Then type the equation using these keys.

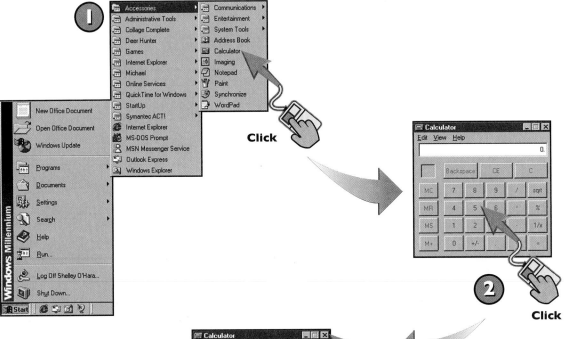

Click

Click

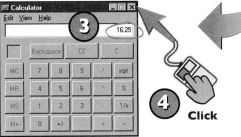

Click

1 Click **Start**, **Programs**, **Accessories**, and then click **Calculator**.

2 Click the buttons on the calculator to enter an equation.

3 You see the results of the calculation.

4 When you are finished, click the **Close** button.

Task 2: Starting WordPad

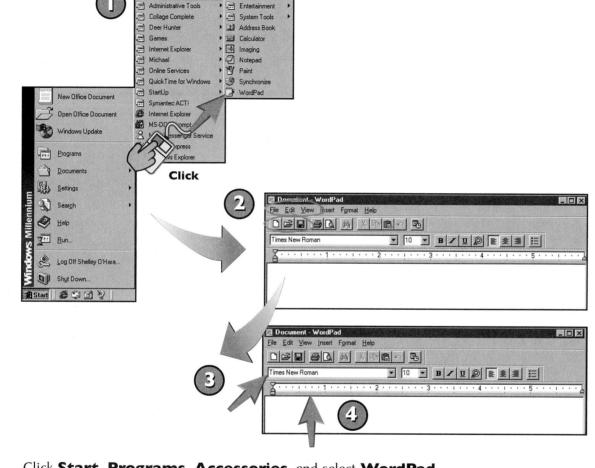

Click

Use WordPad to edit text files or to create simple documents such as notes, memos, fax sheets, and so on. WordPad saves files in Word 6 for Windows format by default, but you can choose to save in a text-only format.

✓ **Maximize the Window**
You can click the **Maximize** button to enlarge the WordPad window and make it easier to work in.

✓ **Hide Toolbars**
To hide any of the screen elements in WordPad, open the **View** menu and click the tool you want to hide. A check mark indicates that the tool is showing; no check mark indicates that it is hidden.

1 Click **Start**, **Programs**, **Accessories**, and select **WordPad**.

2 Use the menu bar to select commands. Use the toolbar to select buttons for frequently used commands.

3 Use the format bar to make changes to the appearance of the text.

4 Use the ruler to set tabs and indents.

Task 3: Typing Text

To create a new document, type the text you want to include. The insertion point indicates where text will be entered as you type.

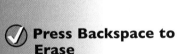

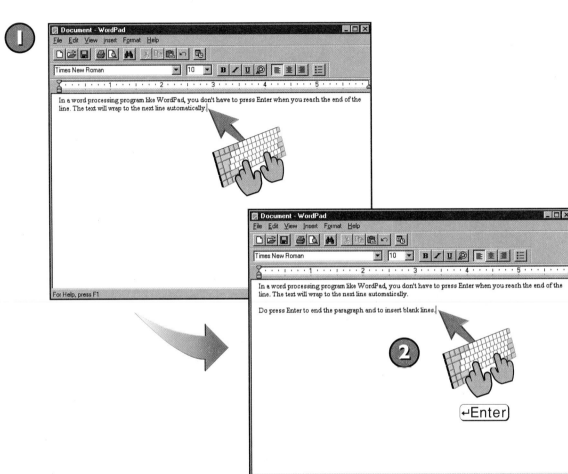

Start Here

Press Backspace to Erase
If you make a mistake while typing, press the **Backspace** key to delete one character at a time. Then retype the text.

Save Your Document
Be sure to periodically save your document. See Task 5, "Saving a Document," in Part 3, "Using Applications in Windows Millennium."

1 Type the text. You don't need to press **Enter** at the end of each line; WordPad automatically wraps the lines within a paragraph.

2 To end a paragraph and start a new one, press **Enter**. The insertion point moves to the next line.

Task 4: Moving Around in a WordPad Document

Start Here

1

> Document - WordPad
> File Edit View Insert Format Help
>
> Times New Roman 10 **B** *I* U
>
> In a word processing program like WordPad, you don't have to press Enter when you reach the end of the line. The text will wrap to the next line automatically.
>
> Do press Enter to end the paragraph and to insert blank lines.
>
> For Help, press F1

Click

To add new text or to select text for editing or formatting, you must know how to move the insertion point to the spot where you want to make a change. You can use either the mouse or the keyboard to move the insertion point.

2

> Document - WordPad
> File Edit View Insert Format Help
>
> Times New Roman 10 **B** *I* U
>
> In a word processing program like WordPad, you don't have to press Enter when you reach the end of the line. The text will wrap to the next line automatically.
>
> Do press Enter to end the paragraph and to insert blank lines.
>
> For Help, press F1

1 Point to the spot in the document where you want to place the insertion point, and click the mouse button.

2 The insertion point moves to that spot.

✓ **Point and Click**
Be sure to both point and click. If you simply point, the insertion point is not moved to the new location.

End Task

One of the greatest things about using a word-processing program, even a simple program such as WordPad, is how easily you can make changes. You can delete text, add text, and more. You can also polish the content of your document, making whatever changes are necessary.

Undo a Change
If you make a mistake, you can undo the last action by clicking the **Edit** menu and choosing **Undo**.

Save Your Work
Be sure to save your document as you continue to work on it. Click **File** and choose **Save** (or click the **Save** button on the toolbar) to save your work. For more information, refer to Task 5, "Saving a Document," in Part 3, "Using Applications in Windows Millennium."

Task 5: Adding Text

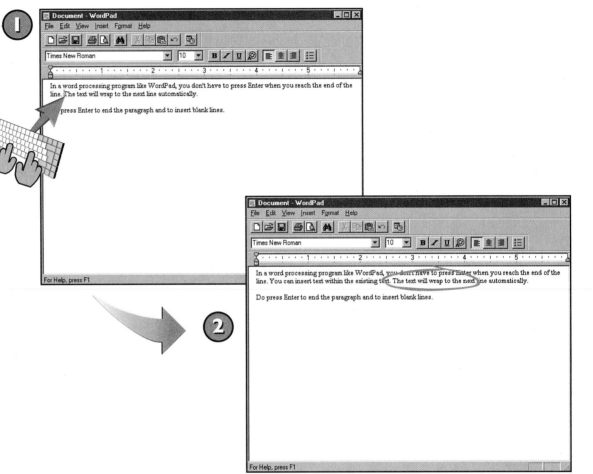

Move the insertion point to the spot where you want to make a change, and start typing.

The existing text moves over to make room.

Task 6: Deleting Text

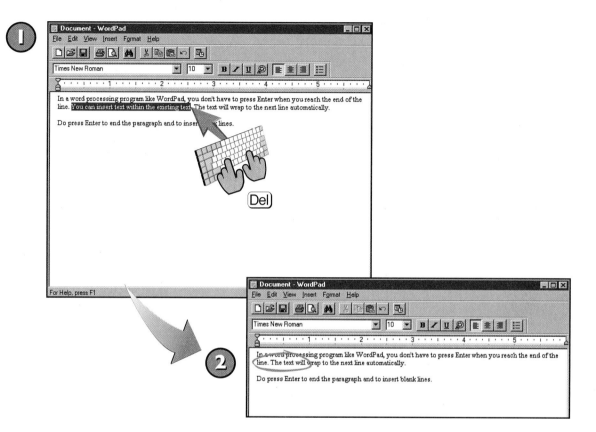

Just as you can add text, you can easily delete it. You can delete characters, words, paragraphs, pages, or even all the text in a document.

Copy or Move Text
For information about selecting, copying, or moving text, refer to Part 3, "Using Applications in Windows Millennium."

Undo Deletion
To undo the deletion, click the **Undo** button in the toolbar.

① Select the text you want to delete, and then press the **Delete** or **Backspace** keys on your keyboard.

② The text is deleted.

Task 7: Formatting Text

You can easily make simple changes to the appearance of the text. For example, you can change the font or font size, and you can make text bold, italic, or underlined. This task touches on just a few of the formatting changes you can make. Experiment to try out some of the other available formatting features.

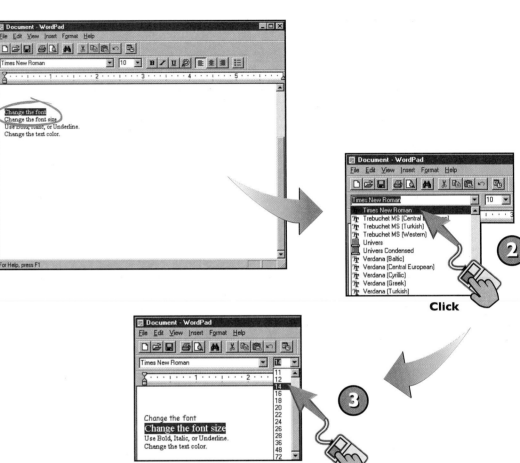

Click

Click

① Select the text you want to change. If you need help selecting text, refer to Task 10, "Selecting Text," in Part 3, "Using Applications in Windows Millennium."

② To use a different font, click the **Font** drop-down arrow and click the font you want.

③ To use a different font size, select the text you want to change, click the **Font Size** drop-down arrow, and click the size you want to use.

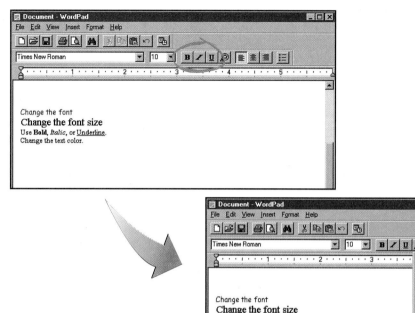

4 To make text bold, italic, or underlined, select the text, and then click the appropriate button in the format bar.

5 To change the font color, select the text you want to change, click the **Font Color** button, and then click the color you want.

Format Paragraphs
You can use toolbar buttons to change many features of the paragraph. For example, use the **Alignment** buttons to change the alignment of the paragraph. Add bullets by clicking the **Bullets** button. To undo a change, click the **Undo** button. You can also use the commands in the **Format** menu to change the appearance of your document.

Save Changes
Save your document by clicking the **Save** button or by clicking **File** and then choosing **Save**. For more information on saving a document, refer to Part 3, "Using Applications in Windows Millennium."

Task 8: Using Notepad

The most common type of simple file is a text file. You can find instructions on how to install a program, beta notes, and other information in text files. Some configuration files are also text files. The icon for this type of file looks like a little notepad, and these files have the extension .TXT. To edit and work with this type of file, you can use Notepad, a simple text editor provided with Windows Millennium.

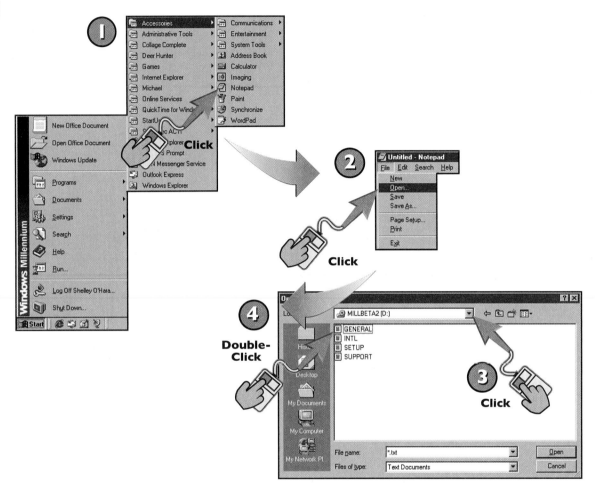

1. Click **Start**, **Programs**, **Accessories**, and then choose **Notepad**.

2. To open a file in Notepad, click **File**, and then choose **Open**.

3. Find the folder that contains your file. You can use the **Look in** drop-down list box to change to a different drive.

4. Double-click the desired file to open it.

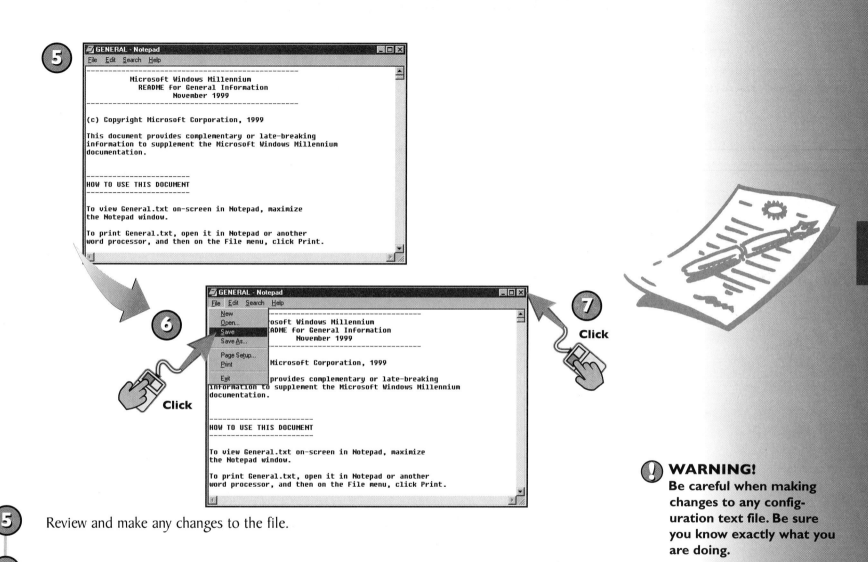

5 Review and make any changes to the file.

6 To save changes to the file, click **File** and then **Save**.

7 To exit Notepad, click the **Close** button.

WARNING!
Be careful when making changes to any configuration text file. Be sure you know exactly what you are doing.

Save Text Files
You can save an edited text file by clicking **File** and choosing **Save**.

End Task

Task 9: Using Paint

Use Paint to create art and to edit graphics such as clip art, scanned art, and art files from other programs. You can add lines, shapes, and colors, as well as alter the original components.

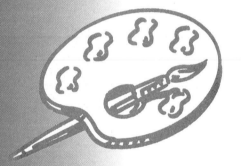

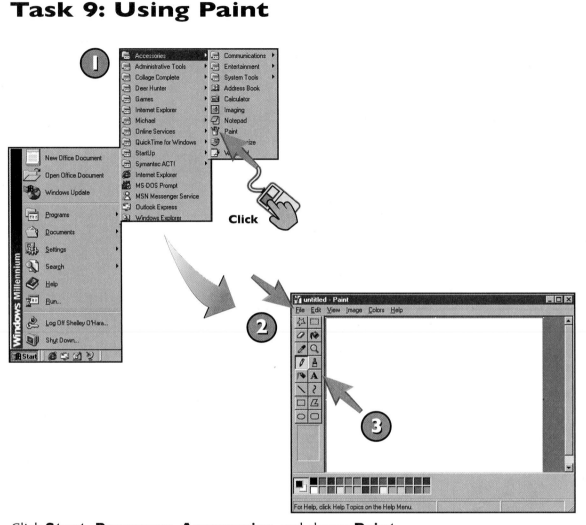

Click **Start**, **Programs**, **Accessories**, and choose **Paint**.

Use the menu bar to select commands.

Use the toolbox to select the drawing tool you want to work with.

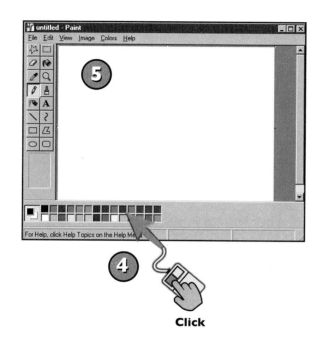

Click

 Use the color box to select colors for the lines and fills of the objects you draw.

Draw in the drawing area.

 Experiment!
You can learn more about Paint by experimenting. Also, use the online help system to look up topics.

Task 10: Drawing a Shape

Using Paint, you can create many different types of shapes, including lines, curves, rectangles, polygons, ovals, circles, and rounded rectangles.

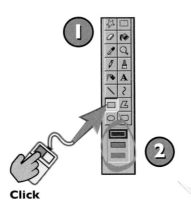

Start Here

Click

✓ **Draw Perfect Shapes**
To draw a circle, square, or straight line, hold down the **Shift** key as you use the **Ellipse**, **Rectangle**, or **Line** tool to draw the object.

✓ **Choose a Color**
You can click in the color bar at the bottom of the Paint window to choose a color. Click the color you want to use for the lines and borders. To select a fill color, right-click the color you want to use.

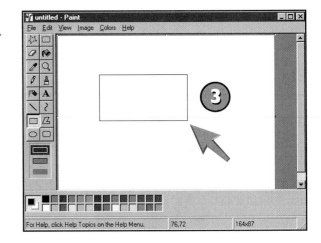

① Click the tool you want to draw with (in this case, the **Rectangle** tool).

✓ **Undo**
If at any time you do not like what you've drawn, open the **Edit** menu and choose **Undo** to undo the last action (or press **Ctrl+Z**).

② The toolbox displays options for the tool you have selected. In this case, choose whether you want to draw an empty rectangle, a filled rectangle with a border, or a filled rectangle without a border.

③ Move the pointer into the drawing area. Click and drag in the white canvas area to draw.

End Task

Task 11: Adding Text to a Drawing

Start Here

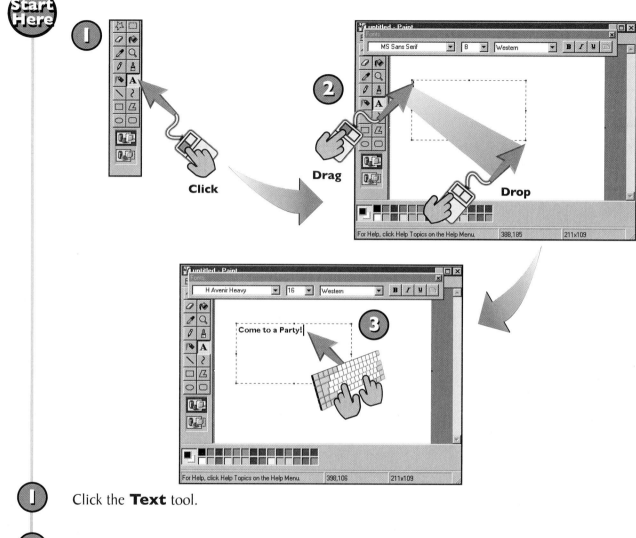

Click

Drag

Drop

You can include text as part of your drawing. To do so, draw a text box, and then type the text you want to include.

1 Click the **Text** tool.

2 Move the pointer into the drawing area. Drag to draw a text box.

3 Type the text you want to add. The text is added to the text box.

✓ **Font Change**
You can use the **Fonts** toolbar to select the font, size, and style of the text.

 End Task

Task 12: Drawing Freehand

In addition to shapes and text, you can also draw freehand on the page. This is similar to drawing with a pencil or pen (only you are drawing in your document using the mouse).

Start Here

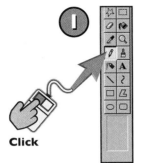

Click

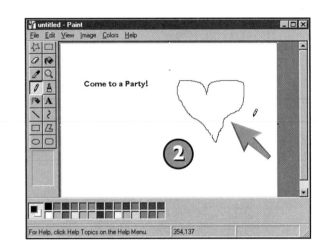

 Click the **Pencil** tool.

 Move the pointer into the drawing area. Hold down the mouse button and drag the pencil icon to draw.

End Task

Task 13: Erasing Part of a Drawing

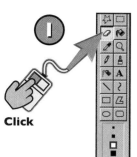

Click

If you make a mistake and want to get rid of something you have added, you can use the **Eraser** tool.

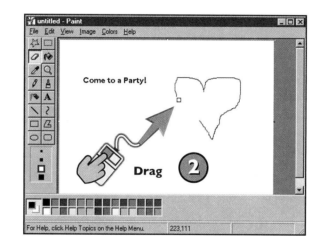

Drag (2)

✓ **Erase Selected Area**
To erase a selected part of a drawing, click the **Select** tool and drag the mouse across part of your drawing. Press the **Delete** key to remove the selected part of the drawing.

① Click the **Eraser** tool.

② Move the pointer to the drawing area. Hold down the mouse button, and drag across the part you want to erase.

✓ **Clear the Whole Page**
To clear everything on the page, click **Image**, and then choose **Clear Image**.

✓ **Size of the Eraser**
You can select the size of the eraser you want to use. Simply click the **Eraser** tool, and then click the size you want to use in the toolbox.

There are many ways to add color to a drawing. One way is to use the **Brush** tool to add paintbrush style strokes to your image.

Task 14: Adding Color to a Drawing Using the Brush Tool

Start Here

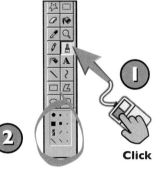

Click

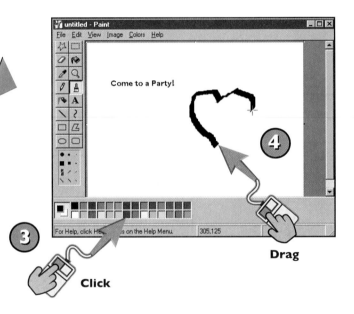

Come to a Party!

Drag

Click

✓ **Brush Styles**
You can select from different brush styles including angled brushes, pointed, or squared tips.

✓ **Spray Paint**
To get a spray-paint effect on the drawing area, use the **Airbrush** tool.

① Click the **Brush** tool.

② Click the brush size and shape.

③ Click the color you want to use in the color box.

④ Hold down the mouse button and drag across the page to "paint" with the brush.

End Task

Task 15: Adding Color to a Drawing Using the Fill with Color Tool

Start Here

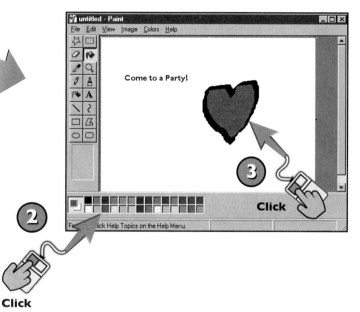

Click

Click

Click

You can use the **Fill with Color** tool to fill an object or drawing area with color. For example, you can fill a rectangle or circle with any of the colors available in the color palette.

1. Click the **Fill with Color** tool.

2. Click the color you want to use.

3. Click inside a closed area you want to paint. That area is filled with the color you selected.

⚠ WARNING!
If color spills outside the area you intended to fill, that probably means you tried to fill an area that was not closed. Be sure that you are filling an area with a border.

End Task

Task 16: Viewing Images

Windows also includes a program that you can use to view graphic files. This program, called Imaging, enables you not only to open and view most types of graphics files, but also to make changes, cropping the image or adding callouts.

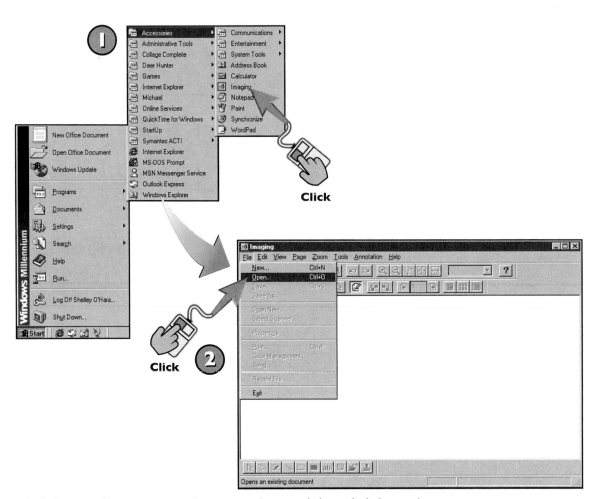

Click

Click **2**

(✓) **My Pictures**
Consider keeping all your graphic files in the **My Pictures** folder. You can then easily find and organize the pictures you have. See Task 3, "Using the My Pictures Folder," in Part 2, "Working with Disks, Folders, and Files."

1 Click **Start**, **Programs**, **Accessories**, and then click **Imaging**.

2 To open a file, click **File**, and then select the **Open** command.

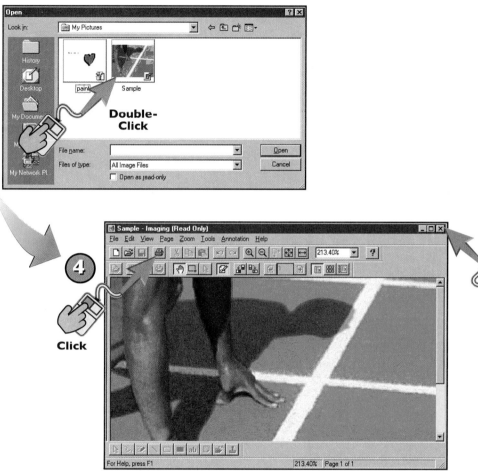

Double-Click

Click

Click

3 Change to the drive and folder that contains the image. Then, when you see the image listed, double-click it.

4 To print the image, click the **Print** button.

5 When you are finished viewing the image, click the **Close** button for the program window.

✓ **Annotate**
You can use the buttons in the Annotation toolbar to add callouts to the image.

⚠ **WARNING!**
If an image is pretty complex, the size of the file is probably large (slowing down your computer). Also, you might find that printing that image takes a long time.

PART 6

Entertainment

Computers are not all work and no fun. Windows Millennium includes entertainment programs for playing CDs, viewing multimedia files, and recording and playing back sounds. You'll also find some games and options for installing and customizing games that are new to Windows Millennium.

Tasks

Task 1: Changing the Volume

If the sound on your PC is too loud or too quiet, you can adjust the volume. To do so, use Volume Control. This feature enables you to set the volume for several types of audio input and output devices.

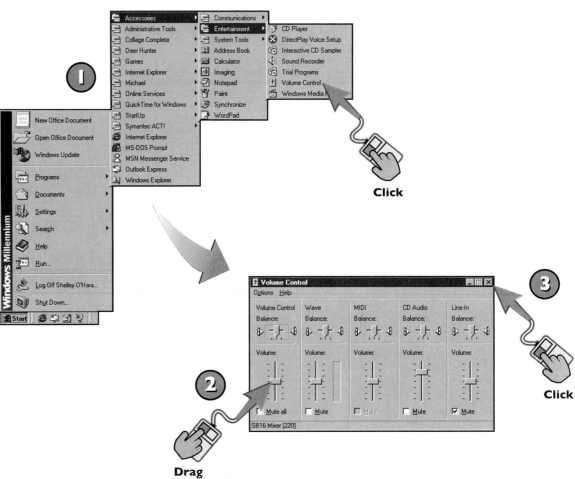

Start Here

Click

Drag

Click

③

② ①

Speaker Volume
You might also have a volume control on your speakers. You can also use these to adjust the sound.

Double-Click Icon
To display the Volume Control panel, you can also double-click the **Speaker** icon in the taskbar.

① Click **Start**, **Programs**, **Accessories**, **Entertainment**, and select **Volume Control**.

② Drag any of the volume control bars in the **Volume Control** window to adjust the volume.

③ Click the **Close** button to close Volume Control.

End Task

Task 2: Playing Games

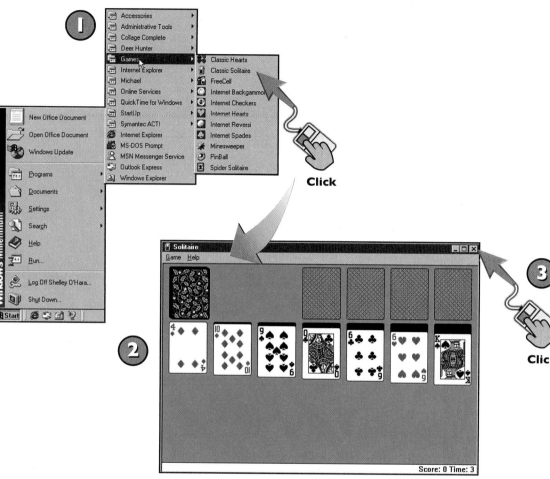

Start Here

Click

Click

Windows provides several games that you can play to break up your workday with a little entertainment. Use any of the games to fill a lunch hour or coffee break and to ease the tensions of the day. Playing games is also a good way to help you get the hang of using the mouse. For example, playing Solitaire can help you practice such mouse skills as clicking, dragging, and so on.

1 Click **Start**, **Programs**, **Games**, and then click the name of the game you want to open (in this case, **Classic Solitaire**).

2 Play the game.

3 When you are finished, click the **Close** button to exit.

✓ No Games?
If you don't see any games listed, they might not have been installed. You can easily add these Windows components to your system (refer to Task 11, "Installing Windows Components," in Part 10, "Setting Up Programs").

✓ Get Help
If you aren't sure how to play a game, get instructions using the online help. Open the **Help** menu and select the **Help** command.

End Task

Task 3: Setting Gaming Options

Often when you play a game you use a special type of controller, such as a gamepad or a flightstick. If you have one of these controllers (or add one later), you can set options for how it works.

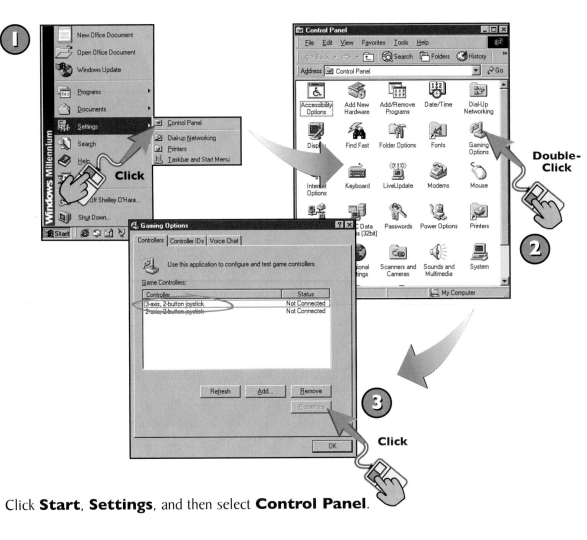

① Click **Start**, **Settings**, and then select **Control Panel**.

② Double-click the **Gaming Options** icon.

③ This screen shows any game controllers attached to your system. Select the controller you want to modify, click **Properties**, and make any changes.

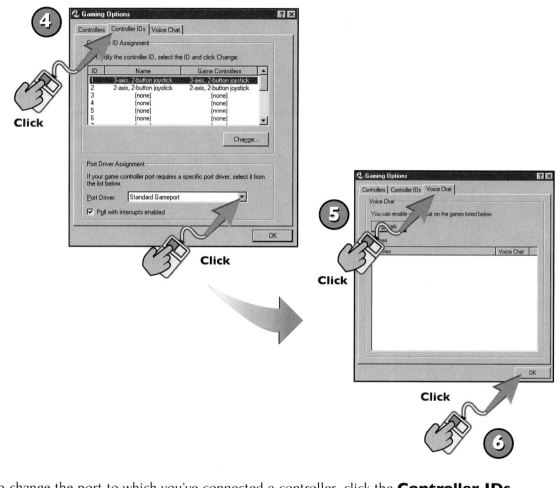

Install Games

The installation of games is also automated with Windows Millennium. You can simply insert the CD, and the game (if the game follows the new guidelines of Windows) will be installed and started without your intervention.

Gaming Options

Some of the options in the **Gaming Options** dialog box are fairly technical. If you aren't sure what an option does, right-click it and select **What's This**.

4. To change the port to which you've connected a controller, click the **Controller IDs** tab. Display the **Port Driver** drop-down list and select the port.

5. Click the **Voice Chat** tab and turn on voice chat for any of the games listed.

6. When you are finished making changes, click **OK**.

Task 4: Playing a Sound with Sound Recorder

You can use Windows multimedia devices, such as the Sound Recorder, to add to the presentations or documents you create in Windows. You can play back sounds recorded and saved as files. You can also use Sound Recorder to record your own sounds and insert the sound files into your documents for clarification or interest. To use the multimedia features of Windows Millennium, you need a sound card and speakers, which are standard on nearly all new computers.

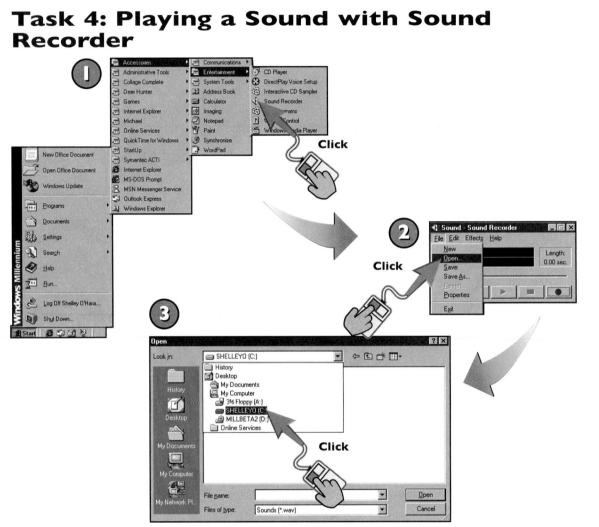

Click **Start**, **Programs**, **Accessories**, **Entertainment**, and select **Sound Recorder**.

The **Sound Recorder** window appears. Click the **File** menu, and then choose **Open**.

From the **Look in** drop-down list, select a folder that contains sound files. (To sample one of the Windows sounds, select the **Windows\Media** folder.)

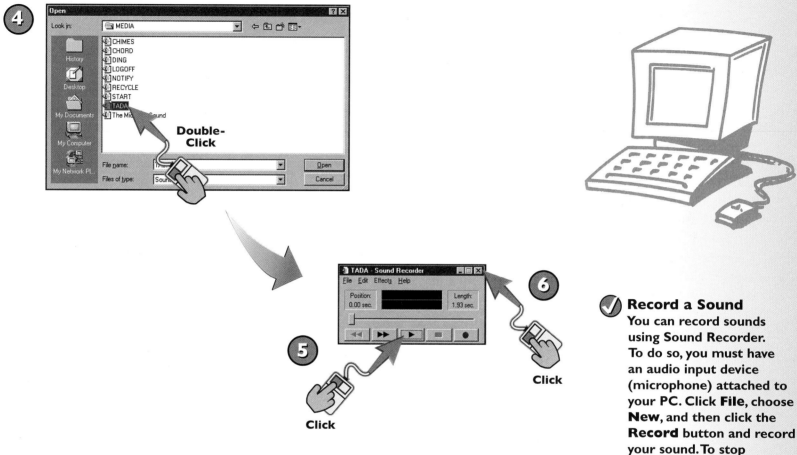

Double-
Click

Click

Click

Record a Sound
You can record sounds using Sound Recorder. To do so, you must have an audio input device (microphone) attached to your PC. Click **File**, choose **New**, and then click the **Record** button and record your sound. To stop recording, click the **Stop** button. To save your sound, click **File**, and then choose **Save As**.

Can't Hear?
If you cannot hear the sound, try adjusting the volume on your speakers.

4   Double-click the sound file you want to play.

5   Click the **Play** button to hear the file.

6   When finished, click the **Close** button to close the **Sound Recorder** window.

Task 5: Playing an Audio CD

In addition to being able to play back sound files, you can play audio CDs using **Windows Media Player**, enabling you to listen to the background music of your choice as you work. **Note that the quality of the playback is determined by the quality of your speakers. Don't expect stereo quality.**

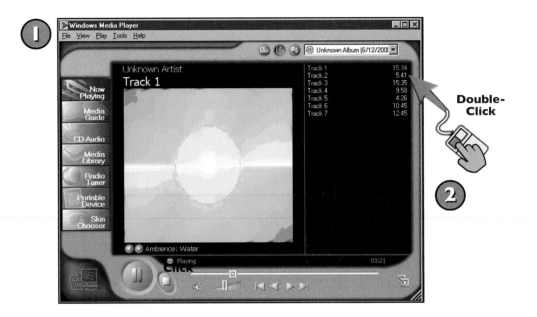

Double-Click

✓ **Didn't Start Automatically?**
If **CD Player** did not start automatically, click **Start, Programs, Accessories,** and then **Entertainment.** Finally, click **CD Player.**

1 Insert the CD into the drive. The CD starts playing automatically.

2 To play a different track, double-click the track from the track list.

Next Step

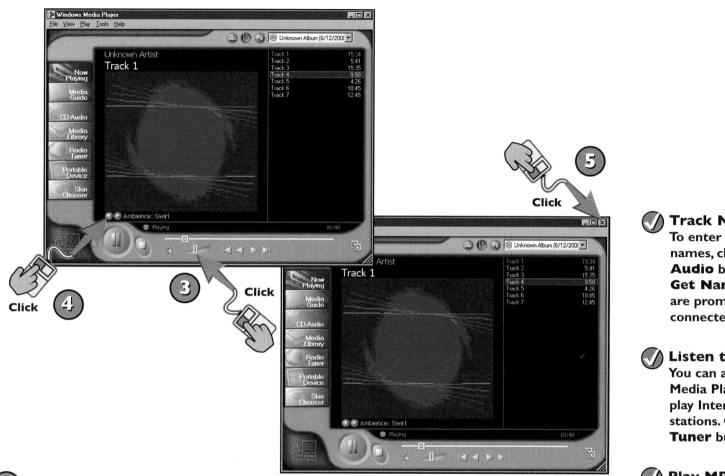

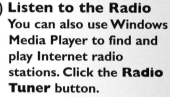

Click

Click

Click

Click

3 To change the volume, drag the volume control.

4 To change the visualization, click the **Next** or **Previous** visualization buttons.

5 When you're finished, click the **Close** button to close the **Windows Media Player** window.

✓ **Track Names**
To enter or download track names, click the **CD Audio** button. Click the **Get Names** button. You are prompted to get connected to the Internet.

✓ **Listen to the Radio**
You can also use Windows Media Player to find and play Internet radio stations. Click the **Radio Tuner** button.

✓ **Play MP3 Files**
You can also sample other music from the Internet. See Part 7, "Connecting to Online Services and the Internet," for more information on finding and listening to music from the Web.

End Task

Task 6: Customizing Windows Media Player

Windows Media Player has been totally revamped. You can use this program to play audio CDs, view media files, and listen to radio stations. You can also copy and manage media.

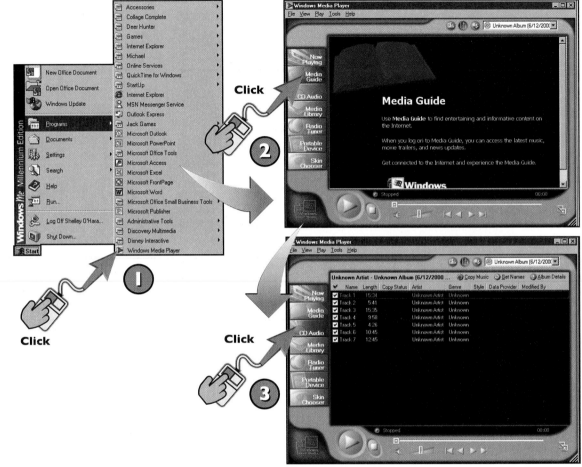

Click

Click

Click

Click **Start**, **Programs**, and select **Windows Media Player**.

Click the **Media Guide** button. You can use this tab to access an online guide of Internet media.

Click the **CD Audio** button. Use these options to view and edit track information for a CD.

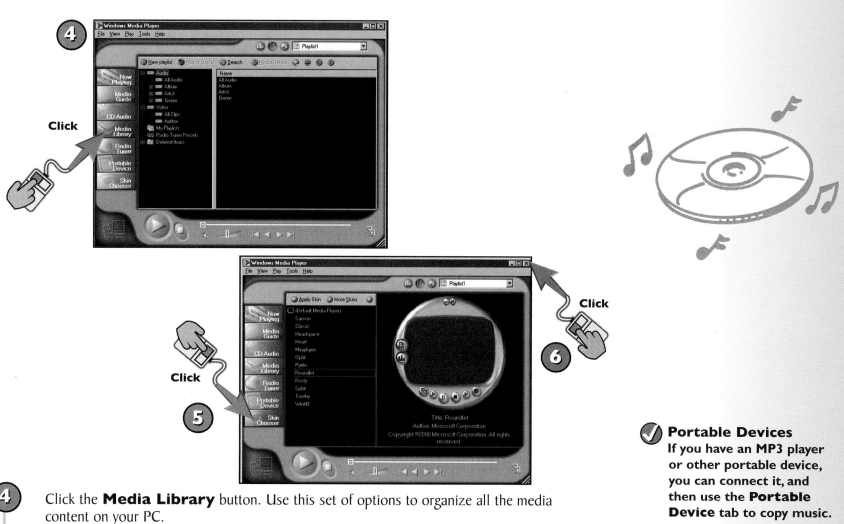

4 Click the **Media Library** button. Use this set of options to organize all the media content on your PC.

5 Click the **Skin Chooser** button, and then select a look for the Windows Media Player program.

6 To close Media Player, click the **Close** button.

 Portable Devices
If you have an MP3 player or other portable device, you can connect it, and then use the **Portable Device** tab to copy music.

 Radio Tuner
Get connected to the Internet, and then access the **Radio Tuner** page to listen to radio stations.

End Task

Connecting to Online Services and the Internet

If you have a modem and an Internet connection, you can venture beyond your PC to resources available from online services, such as America Online and MSN, or from the Internet. Windows Millennium comes with an Online Services folder; you can use the icons in this folder to try out any of these services. Windows Millennium also includes Internet Explorer, a Web browser that offers you complete and convenient browsing of the Internet. As with any browser software, you can use Internet Explorer to view World Wide Web pages, to search for specific topics, and to download and upload files.

Tasks

Task 1: Trying Online Services

Windows Millennium conveniently enables you to try out different online services, including America Online, Prodigy, and AT&T WorldNet. For example, America Online (AOL) is the most popular online service company. AOL provides content, bulletin boards, email, and other services for subscribers. You can also access the Internet through AOL. You can find information and links for getting connected in the **Online Services** folder.

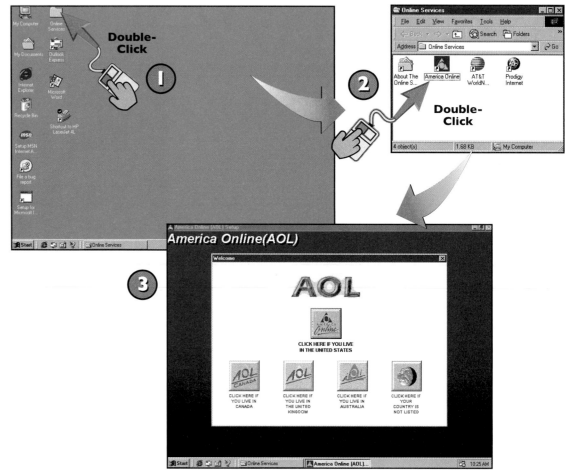

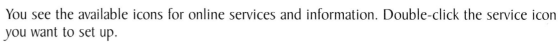

Get Information
To get more information, click the **About The Online Services** icon.

Cancel Setup
You can cancel the setup at any time by clicking the **Cancel** button.

1. Double-click the **Online Services** folder.

2. You see the available icons for online services and information. Double-click the service icon you want to set up.

3. Follow the onscreen instructions.

Page 136

Task 2: Trying MSN

Start Here

Double-Click

Welcome to MSN Internet Access!

Get fast, reliable Internet Access and e-mail from Microsoft

We'll now guide you through the setup process.
Note: This process is for both new and existing MSN members.

Please click Next to continue.

Cancel   Next ►

In addition to the other services in the **Online Services** folder, you can also use **MSN**, Microsoft's online service (similar in content to America Online). You can find a link for getting set up for this service on the desktop.

Double-click the **Setup MSN Internet Access** icon.

Follow the onscreen instructions for getting set up.

✓ **Have Your Disk**
You might be prompted to insert your Windows Millennium disc. Be sure you have it handy.

Task 3: Starting Internet Explorer

Start Here

After you've set up your Internet connection, you can start Internet Explorer and browse the Internet. To start, take a look at the different tools for browsing the Web.

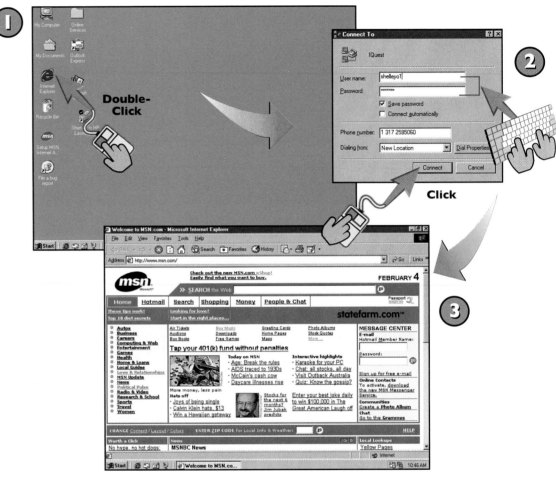

Double-Click

Click

① Use the Toolbar
You can also click the **Launch Internet Explorer Browser** button in the Quick Launch toolbar (found in the taskbar) to start Internet Explorer.

② Trouble Connecting?
If you have problems connecting—the line is busy, for example—try again. If you continue to have problems, check with your ISP.

① Double-click the **Internet Explorer** icon.

② Enter your user name and password (some information might have been completed for you), and then click the **Connect** button.

③ Windows connects to your ISP. The Internet Explorer window appears, and you see your start page, usually the MSN home page.

End Task

Task 4: Typing an Address

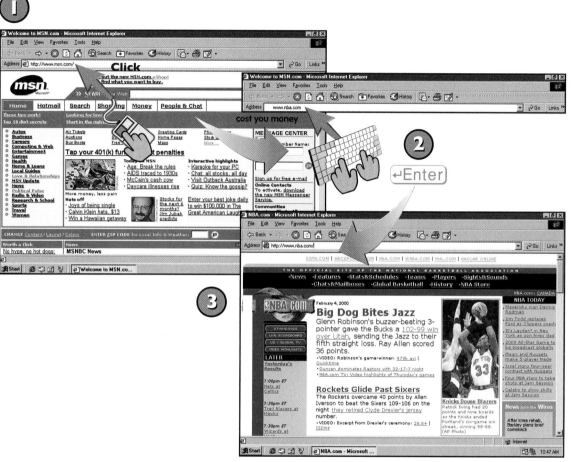

Typing a site's address is the fastest way to get to that site. An address, or URL (uniform resource locator), consists of the protocol (usually `http://`) and the domain name (something like `www.nba.com`). The domain name might also include a path (a list of folders) to the document. The extension (usually `.com`, `.net`, `.gov`, `.edu`, or `.mil`) indicates the type of site (commercial, network resources, government, educational, or military, respectively).

✅ **Type the Address Correctly**
Make sure you type the address correctly. You must type the periods, colons, slashes, and other characters in the exact order.

✅ **Use AutoComplete**
If you have typed a specific address before, you can type only its first few letters; Internet Explorer will display the rest.

① Click in the **Address** bar.

② Type the address of the site you want to visit, and then press **Enter**.

③ Internet Explorer displays the page for that address.

Information on the Internet is easy to browse because documents contain links to other pages, documents, and sites. Simply click a link to view the associated page. You can jump from link to link, exploring all types of topics and levels of information. Links are also called *hyperlinks*, and usually appear underlined and sometimes in a different color. You can also use the buttons in the toolbar to navigate from page to page.

Task 5: Browsing with Links and Toolbar Buttons

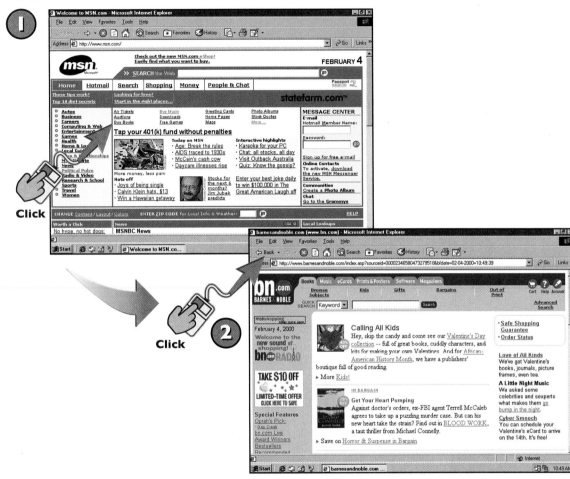

Click

Click

① Click a link. Here you see the MSN start page. You can click the **Buy Books** link.

② The page for that link appears (in this case, barnesandnoble.com). Click the **Back** button in the toolbar to go to the last page you visited.

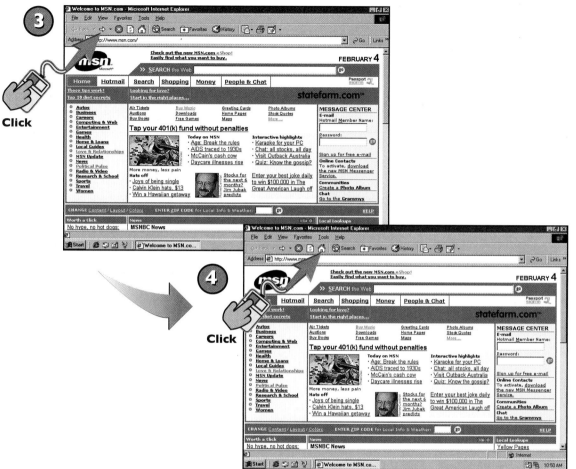

 Click

Click

3 Click the **Forward** button to move forward through the pages you've already visited (you must have clicked the **Back** button before you can use the **Forward** button).

4 To return to the MSN start page, click the **Home** button in the toolbar.

✅ **Error?**
If you see an error message when you click a link, it could indicate that the link is not accurate or that the server is too busy. Try again later.

✅ **Image Links**
Images can serve as links. You can tell whether an image (or text) is a link by placing your mouse pointer on it. If the pointer changes into a pointing hand, the image (or text) is a link.

End Task

Task 6: Searching the Internet

The Internet includes many, many, many different sites. Looking for the site you want by browsing can be like looking for a needle in a haystack. Instead, you can search for a topic and find all sites related to that topic.

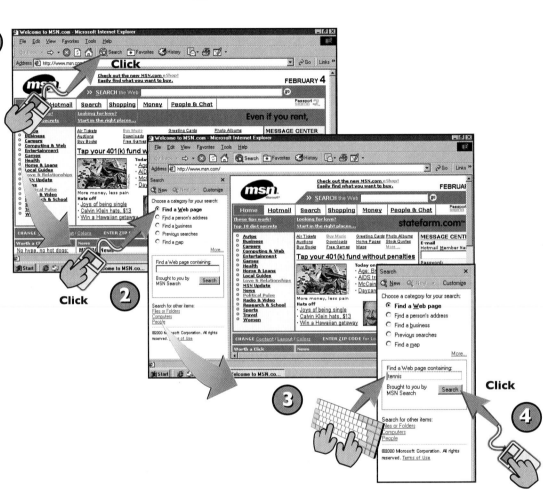

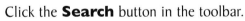

Click

Click

Click

1 Click the **Search** button in the toolbar.

2 You see the Search pane. Select what you want to find (here a Web page).

3 Type the word or phrase you want to find.

4 Click the **Search** button.

Next Step

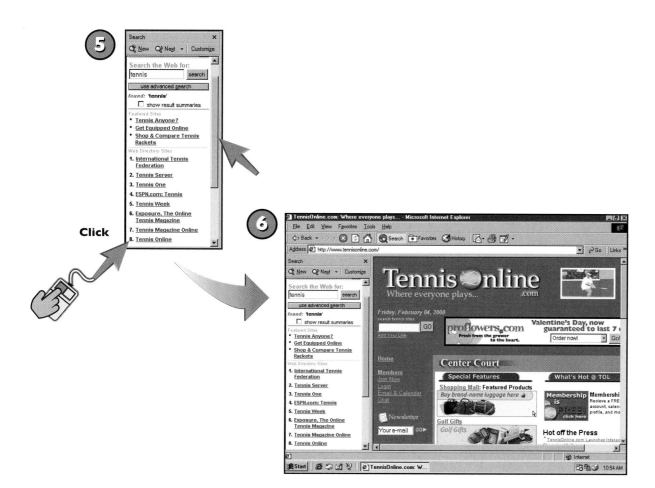

Click

The left pane displays the results of the search in link format. Scroll down until you find the link you want, and then click it.

The page you selected appears in the right pane.

✅ **Use Advanced Search**
You can refine a search and set search options, such as which search tools are used. To do so, click the **use advanced search** button.

✅ **Scroll Through Results**
You can scroll through the Search bar to see all the results. To close the Search bar, click its **Close** button.

End Task

When you find a site that
you especially like, you
might want a quick way to
return to it without having
to browse from link to link
or having to remember the
address. Fortunately,
Internet Explorer enables
you to build a list of favorite
sites and to access those
sites by clicking them in
the list.

Task 7: Adding a Site to Your Favorites List

Click

Click

Click

✅ **Add to a Folder**
You can add the site to a
folder you have set up
(covered in Task 9,
"Rearranging Your
Favorites List"). To do so,
click the **Create in** button,
and then select the folder
in which to place the link.

① Display the Web site that you want to add to your **Favorites** list, and click the **Favorites** menu (do not click the **Favorites** button in the toolbar).

② Click the **Add to Favorites** command.

③ Type a name for the page (if you're not satisfied with the default name that is provided).

④ Click **OK** to save the page in your **Favorites** list.

Task 8: Going to a Site in Your Favorites List

Start Here

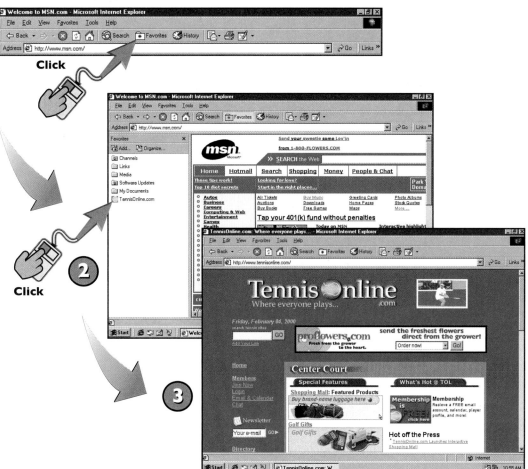

After you have added a site to your **Favorites** list, you can easily reach that site by displaying the list and selecting the site.

Click

Click

(1) Click the **Favorites** button on the toolbar.

(2) The pane on the left side of the screen contains your **Favorites** list, while the right pane contains the current page. Click the site you want to visit.

(3) Internet Explorer displays the site you selected from the **Favorites** list.

 Close List
To close the **Favorites** list, click its **Close** button.

 Use Menu
You can also reach a site by opening the **Favorites** menu and selecting the site from the list.

 End Task

Task 9: Rearranging Your Favorites List

If you add several sites to your **Favorites** list, it might become difficult to use. You can organize the list by grouping similar sites together in a folder. You can add new folders and move sites from one folder to another to keep your favorites from getting cluttered.

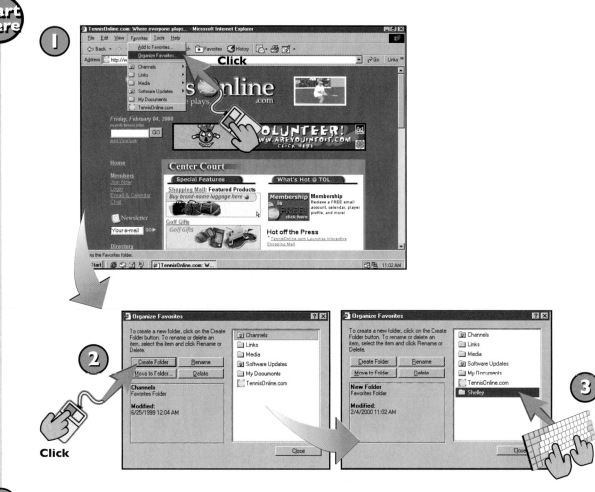

Click

Click

Open the **Favorites** menu, and then choose **Organize Favorites**.

To create a new folder, click the **Create Folder** button.

Type the folder name and press **Enter**.

Rename Site in List
To rename a site, select the site and click the **Rename** button. Type a new name, and press **Enter**.

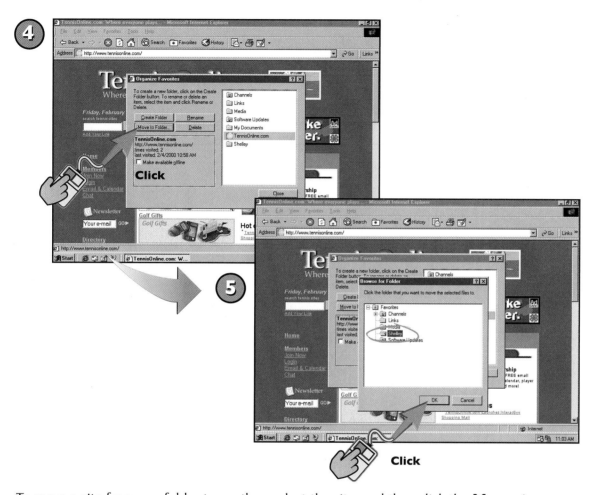

Click

Click

 To move a site from one folder to another, select the site, and then click the **Move to Folder** button.

 Select the folder to which you want to move the site, and then click **OK**. The site will now be located in its assigned folder.

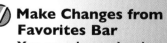 **Delete Site from List**
To delete a site, select it and click the **Delete** button. Click the **Yes** button to confirm the deletion.

Make Changes from Favorites Bar
You can also make changes while the **Favorites** bar is displayed. Click the **Organize** button in the **Favorites** bar.

End Task

Task 10: Using the History List

As you browse from link to link, you might remember a site that you liked, but not remember that site's name or address. You can easily return to sites you have visited by displaying the **History** list. From this list, you can select the week and day you want to review, and then the site you want to visit.

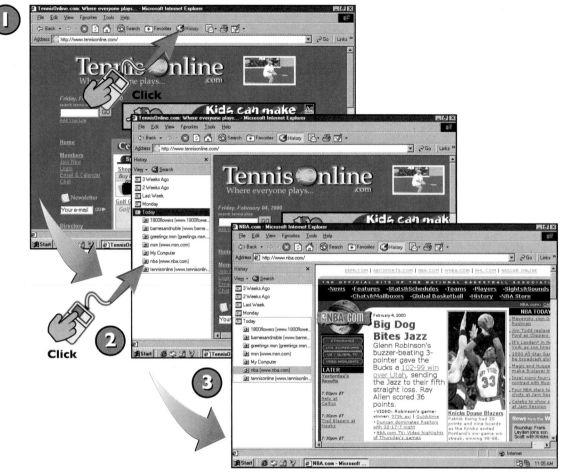

✓ **Close List**
To close the **History** list, click the **Close** button in the top-right corner of the **History** bar.

✓ **How Long Saved?**
You can select how many days the history is kept, and you can clear the **History** list. Choose **Tools**, click **Internet Options**, and then select the number of days the history should be kept. To clear the history, click the **Clear History** button.

① Click the **History** button.

② Internet Explorer displays the **History** list. If necessary, select the week whose list you want to review, and then click the site and page you want to visit.

③ Internet Explorer displays that site.

Task 11: Setting Your Home Page

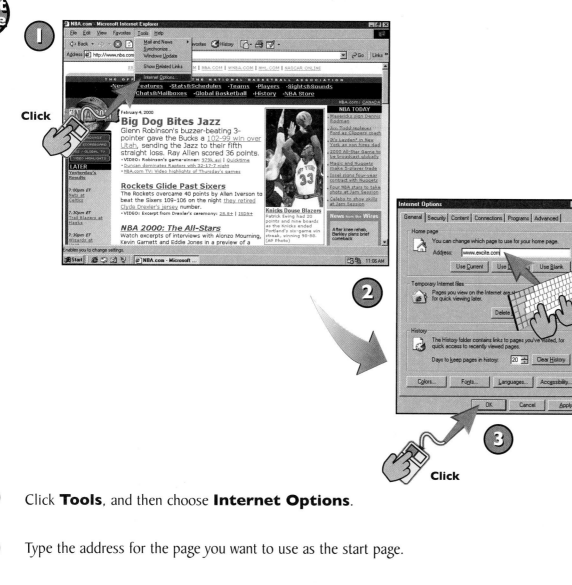

Click

Click

When you click the **Home** button, Internet Explorer displays your home or start page. You don't have to use the page that is selected; you can use any page as your start page.

①
Click **Tools**, and then choose **Internet Options**.

②
Type the address for the page you want to use as the start page.

③
Click **OK**.

✓ Use the Default
To go back to the default page, follow the same steps, but click the **Use Default** button.

✓ Use Current
Rather than type the address, you can display the page you want to use. Select **View, Internet Options**, and then click the **Use Current** button.

Task 12: Setting Internet Security Levels

With Internet Explorer, you can assign different zones to various sites and assign a security level to each zone. Assign the **Local** zone to sites on your intranet; assign the **Trusted** zone to any sites from which it is safe to download and run files; assign the **Restricted** zone to sites from which it is not safe to download and run files. The **Internet** zone is assigned to all other sites by default. A site's assigned zone is displayed in the status bar.

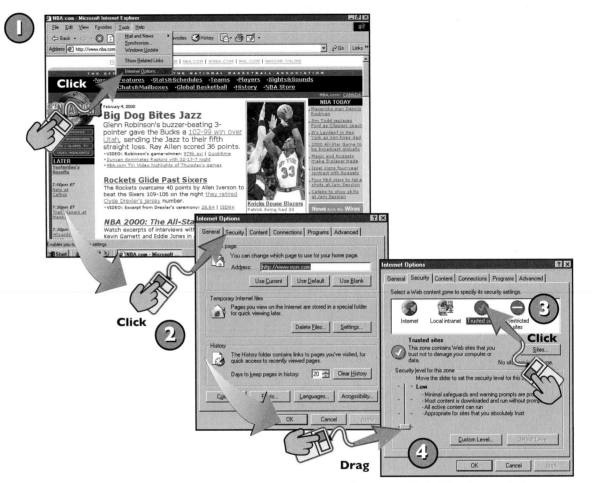

1. To view information about zones or to alter the settings of a zone, click **Tools**, and then choose **Internet Options**.

2. Click the **Security** tab in the **Internet Options** dialog box.

3. To set the security level for a zone, select it in the **Select a Web content zone...** area.

4. Select **High**, **Medium**, **Low**, or **Custom** on the **Security level for this zone** slider bar to set that zone's level of security.

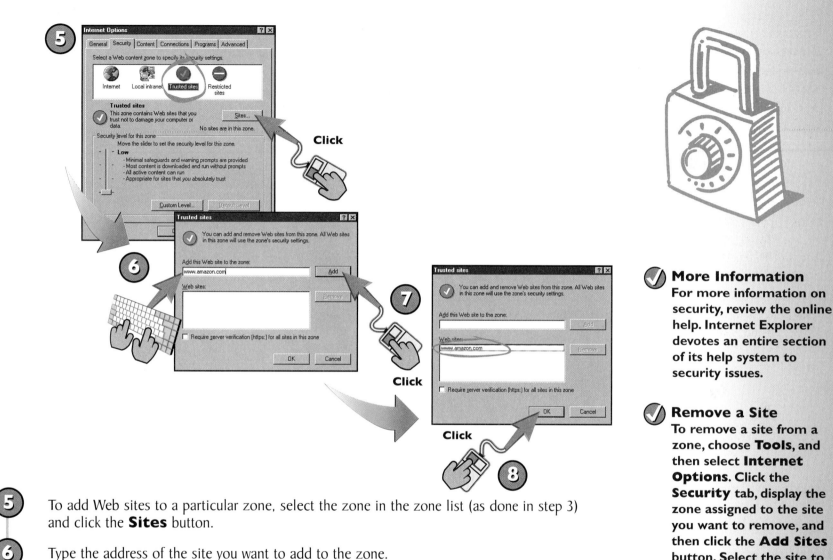

Click

Click

Click

More Information
For more information on security, review the online help. Internet Explorer devotes an entire section of its help system to security issues.

Remove a Site
To remove a site from a zone, choose **Tools**, and then select **Internet Options**. Click the **Security** tab, display the zone assigned to the site you want to remove, and then click the **Add Sites** button. Select the site to be removed and click the **Remove** button. Click **OK** twice to exit the dialog boxes.

5 To add Web sites to a particular zone, select the zone in the zone list (as done in step 3) and click the **Sites** button.

6 Type the address of the site you want to add to the zone.

7 Click the **Add** button (Internet Explorer will add the site).

8 The site is added. Do this for each site you want to add. Then click **OK**. Click **OK** again to close the **Internet Options** dialog box.

Task 13: Exiting Internet Explorer

When you are finished browsing the Internet, you must exit Internet Explorer and also end your connection to your Internet provider.

 Start Here

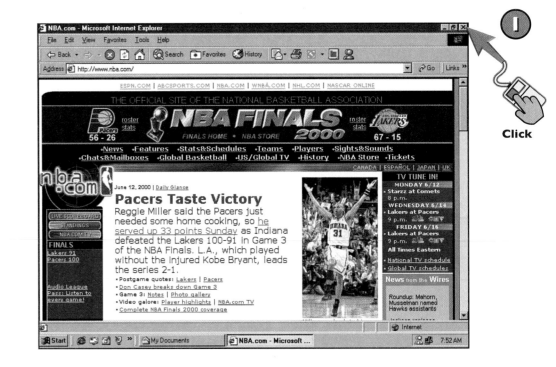

 **1** Click

 How to Log Off
You might be prompted to log off your ISP connection. If so, simply select the **Disconnect** option. If not, right-click the connection icon in the taskbar, and then select **Disconnect**.

1 To exit, click the **Close** button in the upper-right corner of the Internet Explorer window.

 Next Step

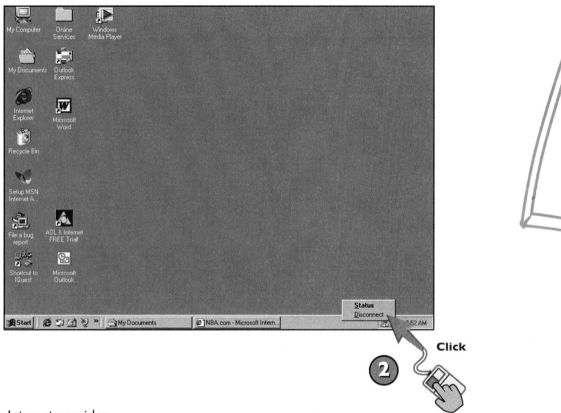

Click

 Log off your Internet provider.

Communicating with Email and Newsgroups

Probably the most popular Internet activity is the sending and receiving of email (electronic messages). Included with Internet Explorer is a mail program, Outlook Express, which you can use to send and receive messages. You can also use this program to participate in newsgroups, which are forums for online discussions. This part covers the key email and newsgroup tasks using Outlook Express.

Tasks

Task 1: Starting Outlook Express

You can use Outlook Express to create, send, and receive email over the Internet. You can also send files by attaching them to your messages.

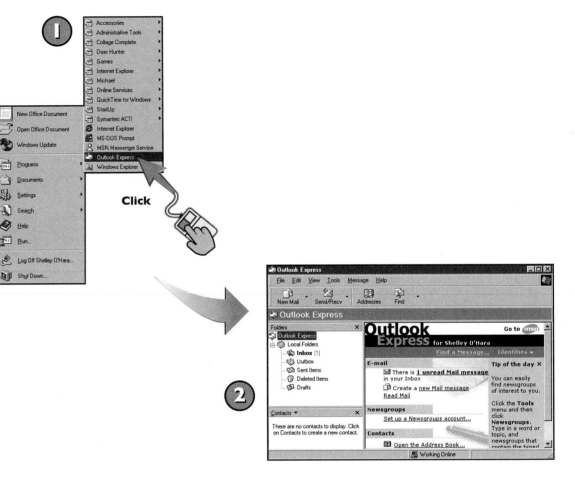

Click

✓ Not Set Up?
If you have not yet set up a mail account, you will be prompted to do so. Follow the onscreen instructions, entering the appropriate user name, password, and mail information from your Internet service provider.

✓ Other Ways to Start
To start Outlook Express from Internet Explorer, click the **Mail** button and choose **Read Mail**. To start Outlook Express from the Quick Launch toolbar, click the **Launch Outlook Express** button.

1 Click **Start**, choose the **Programs** command, and then click **Outlook Express**.

2 Outlook Express starts.

End Task

Task 2: Reading Mail

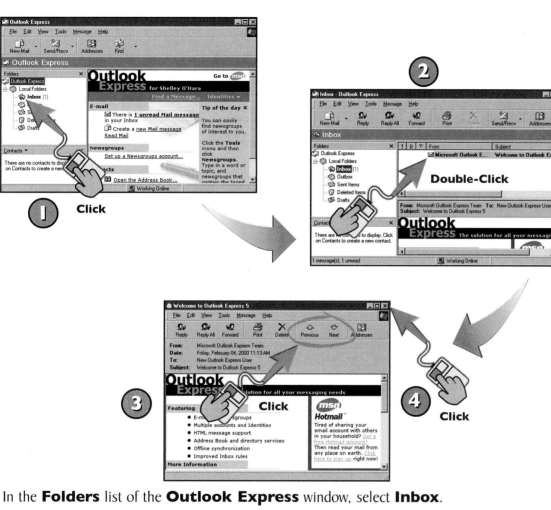

Click

Double-Click

Click

Click

When you start Outlook Express and connect with your ISP, the messages are downloaded from your Internet mail server to your computer. The number of messages in your inbox appears in parentheses next to the inbox in the folder list (the pane on the left side of the screen). When you display your inbox, the message list (the upper-right pane) lists all messages. Messages appearing in bold have not yet been read, but you can open and read any message in the message list.

✓ **Check Mail**
To check your mail manually, click the **Send/Recv** button in the Outlook window.

✓ **Print a Message**
To print an open message, choose **File**, select **Print**, and then click **OK** in the **Print** dialog box.

① In the **Folders** list of the **Outlook Express** window, select **Inbox**.

② Double-click the message you want to read.

③ The message you selected is displayed in its own window. You can display the previous or next message in the list with the **Previous** and **Next** arrows in the toolbar.

④ To close the message, click the **Close** button.

8

Task 3: Responding to Mail

You can easily respond to a message you've received. Outlook Express completes the address and subject lines for you; you can then simply type the response.

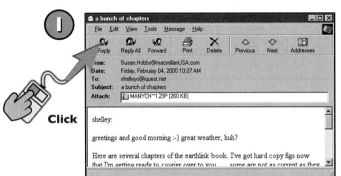

Click

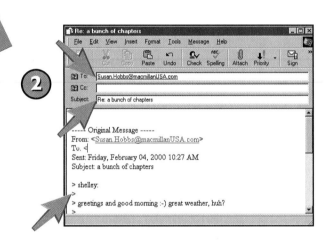

✓ Wrong Address?
If you enter an incorrect address and the message is not sent, you most likely will receive a Failure to Deliver notice. Be sure to type the address in its proper format.

 Display the message to which you want to reply, and click the **Reply** button in the toolbar.

 The address and subject lines are completed, and the text of the original message is appended to the bottom of the reply message.

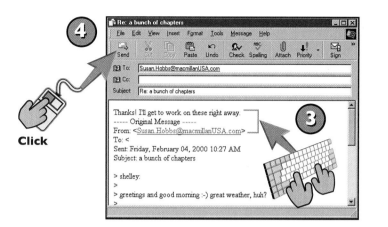

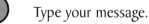
Click

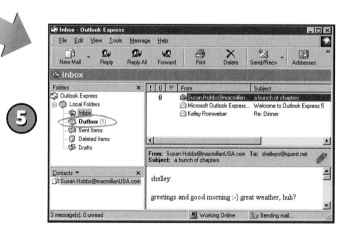

Forward a Message
To forward a message, click the **Forward** command in the **Message** menu or click the **Forward** button. Type the address of the recipient, and then click in the message area and type any message you want to include. Then click the **Send** button.

Reply to All
If the message was sent to several people (for example, cc'd to others), you can reply to all the recipients. Click the **Reply All** button, type the message, and then click **Send**.

3 Type your message.

4 Click the **Send** button.

5 The message is placed in your **Outbox** and then sent.

Task 4: Creating and Sending New Mail

You can send a message to anyone with an Internet email address. Simply type the recipient's email address, a subject, and the message. You can also send carbon copies (Cc) and blind carbon copies (Bcc) of messages, as well as attach files to your messages.

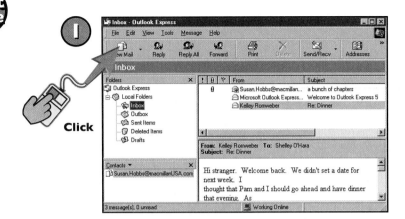

Click

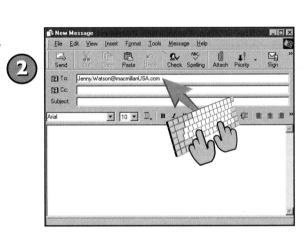

In the **Outlook Express** window, click the **New Mail** button.

Type the recipient's address (as well any necessary Cc and Bcc addresses). Addresses are in the format username@domainname.ext (for example, sohara@msn.com). Press **Tab**.

Next Step

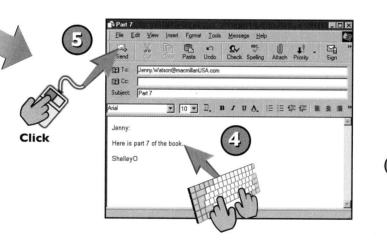

Click

Type a subject in the **Subject** text box, and then press **Tab**.

Type your message.

When you've completed the message, click the **Send** button.

Task 5: Setting Email Preferences

Outlook Express uses certain defaults for how messages are handled when you create, send, and receive them. You can check out these settings, and if necessary, make any changes.

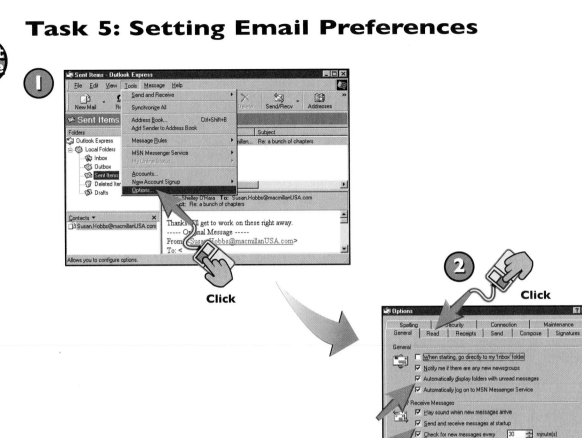

Click

Click

In the **Outlook Express** window, click **Tools**, and then choose **Options**.

On the **General** tab, make changes to options such as whether the **Inbox** is automatically displayed, how often messages are checked, and so on. Click the **Read** tab.

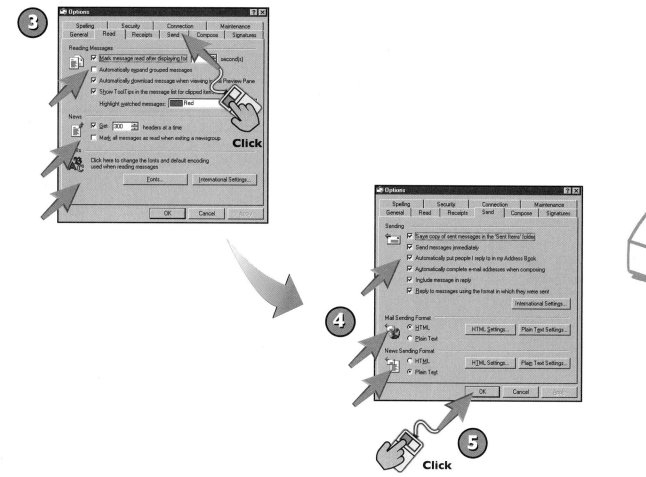

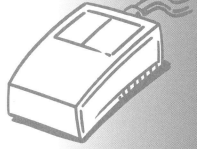

Click

Click

 Make changes to how new messages are handled, and click the **Send** tab.

 Make changes to how sent items are handled.

5 When you're finished making changes, click the **OK** button.

✅ **Other Tabs**
The **Options** dialog box includes several other tabs for making changes. You can click and review the options on these tabs as well.

Task 6: Adding Addresses to Your Address Book

If you often send email to one person you don't want to type the address each time. Instead, you can add the name to your **Address Book.** Then you can quickly select this name and address when creating new messages or forwarding messages. The fastest way to add an address is to pick it up from an existing message.

Start Here

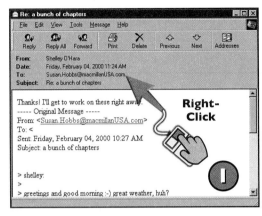

Right-Click

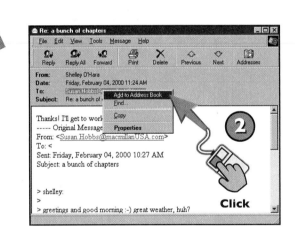

Click

① Display a message to or from the person you want to add, and right-click their email address.

② In the menu that appears, click **Add to Address Book**.

Next Step

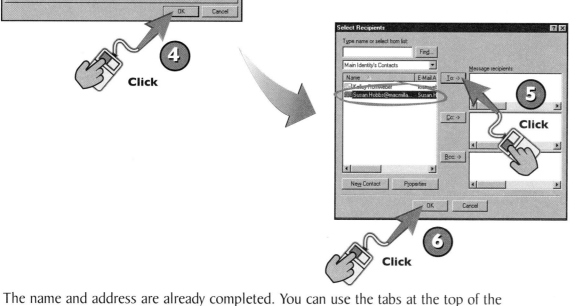

Click

Click

Click

3 The name and address are already completed. You can use the tabs at the top of the window to enter information for this contact (but you don't have to).

4 Click **OK**.

5 To select an address from the address list, click the **To** button in a message window. You see the **Address Book**. Select the person to add, and click **To**.

6 Click **OK**.

Right-Click Sender
You can also right-click a message from that sender and select **Add Sender to Address Book**.

New Address
If you don't have a message, you can manually add a person to the **Address Book**. Click **Addresses** in the **Outlook Express** window. Then click **New** and select **New Contact**. Complete the information for that person, and click **OK**.

Task 7: Looking Up Email Addresses

If you don't know a person's email address, you can use any one of several Web directories to try to find that address.

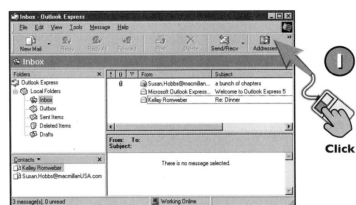

Click

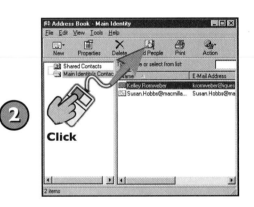

Click

1. In the **Outlook Express** window, click the **Addresses** button.

2. In the **Address Book**, click the **Find People** button.

Next Step

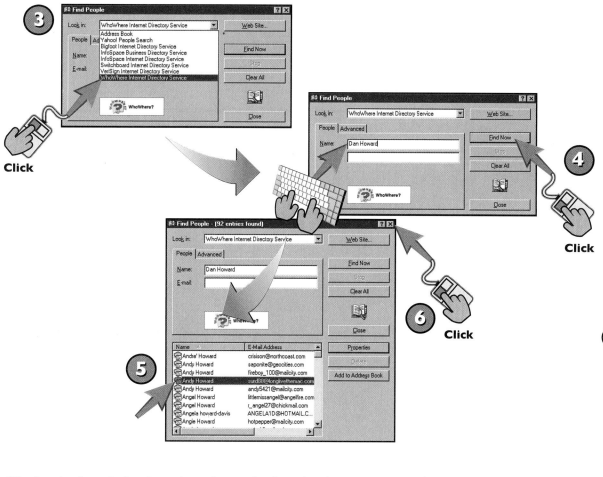

Click

Click

Click

End Task

③ Display the **Look in** drop-down list and select the directory to search.

④ Type the person's name, and click **Find Now**.

⑤ You see a list of matches. You can review this list to find the person you are seeking.

⑥ To close the list, click the **Close** button.

✓ No Matches?
Just because you don't find a match, doesn't mean that person doesn't have email. That person might not be listed in that particular directory. Try another directory.

✓ Right Person?
You might find several matches. Be sure you have the right person. You can get more information about a match by selecting it and clicking the **Properties** button.

Task 8: Subscribing to Newsgroups

A *newsgroup* is a collection of messages on the Internet relating to a particular topic. Anyone can post a message, and anyone who subscribes to the newsgroup can view and respond to posted messages. You can join any of hundreds of thousands of newsgroups on the Internet to exchange information and learn about hobbies, businesses, pets, computers, people of different walks of life, and more. You can use Outlook Express for both email and newsgroups.

✓ **No News Server Listed?**
If a news server is not listed, you have not set up your news account. Use the **Tools**, **Accounts** command to set up your server.

✓ **First Time?**
The first time you select your newsgroup, you see a dialog box asking whether you want to view a list of the available newsgroups. Follow the onscreen instructions for viewing and subscribing to a newsgroup.

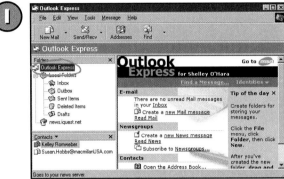

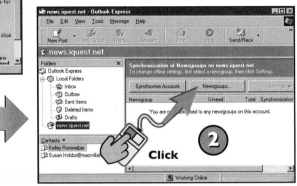

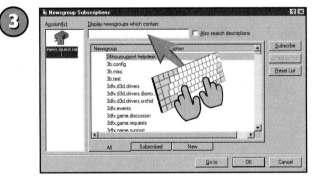

In the **Outlook Express** folder list, click your news server.

Click the **Newsgroups** button to subscribe to a newsgroup.

In the **Display newsgroups which contain:** text box, type the name of a topic area that interests you.

Next Step

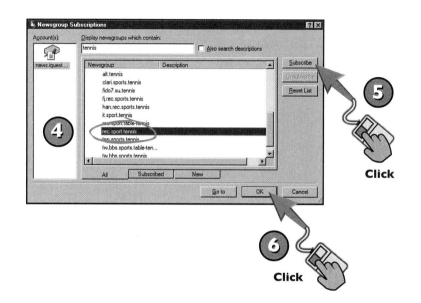

Click

Click

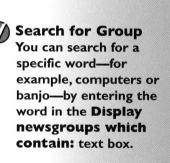

(4) Select a newsgroup that interests you from the **Newsgroup** list (I typed `tennis` for my subject, so the list reflects this choice).

(5) Click the **Subscribe** button.

(6) Click **OK**.

Search for Group
You can search for a specific word—for example, computers or banjo—by entering the word in the **Display newsgroups which contain:** text box.

Unsubscribe
To unsubscribe to a newsgroup, click the **Newsgroups** button. Select the newsgroup to which you want to unsubscribe, and then click the **Unsubscribe** button.

Task 9: Reading Newsgroup Messages

After you have subscribed to a newsgroup, you can review any of the messages in that group. When a new message is posted, it starts a thread, and all responses are part of this thread. You can review all the current messages in the thread.

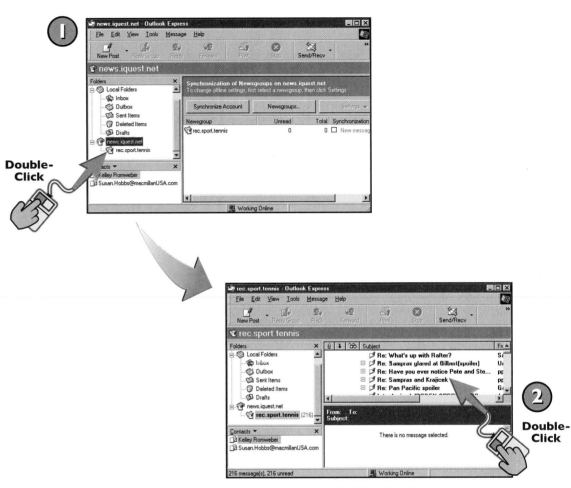

Start Here

Double-Click

Double-Click

In the folder list of the **Outlook Express** window, double-click the newsgroup you want to review.

A list of that newsgroup's messages appears in the message list. Messages in bold have not yet been read; messages with a plus sign have responses. Double-click the message you want to read.

Next Step

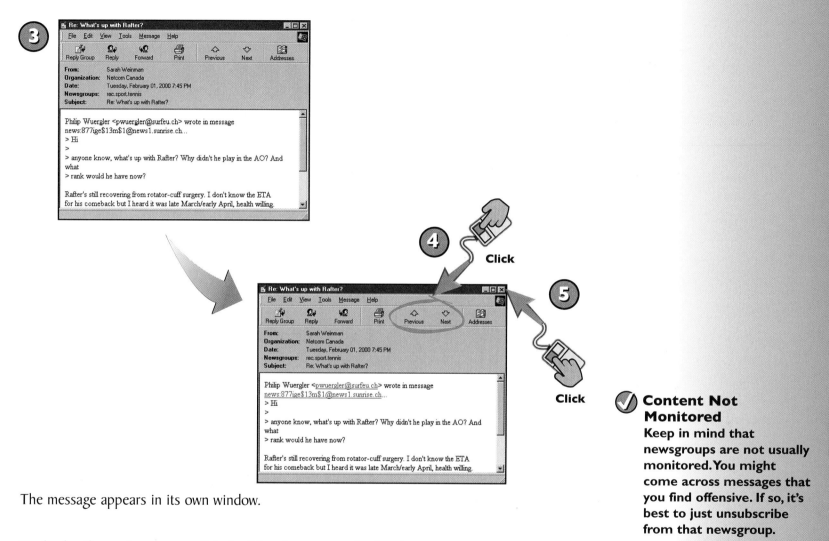

Click

Click

3 The message appears in its own window.

4 To display the next message, click the **Next** arrow; to display the previous message, click the **Previous** arrow.

5 To close the message, click the **Close** button.

✓ Content Not Monitored
Keep in mind that newsgroups are not usually monitored. You might come across messages that you find offensive. If so, it's best to just unsubscribe from that newsgroup.

✓ Print a Message
To print a message, select it in the window, click **File**, and choose **Print**.

Task 10: Posting New Messages

After you review messages, you might want to post some thoughts of your own. One way to do this is to post a new message or start a new thread.

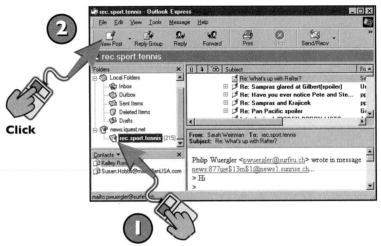

Click

Click

In the **Folders** list, select the newsgroup to which you want to post a new message.

Click the **New Post** button.

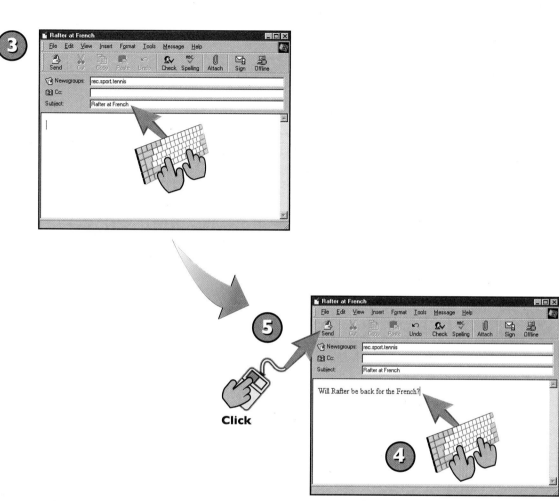

3 Type a subject in the subject line of the **New Message** dialog.

4 Type your message.

5 Click the **Send** button on the toolbar.

✓ Stop Message?
If you change your mind about posting a message, you can cancel the message if you have not already clicked **Send**. Simply click the message's **Close** button and, when prompted, click the **Yes** button to confirm that you don't want to save the message.

If you come across a newsgroup message to which you want to respond, you can post a reply to that message.

Task 11: Replying to an Existing Newsgroup Message

Start Here

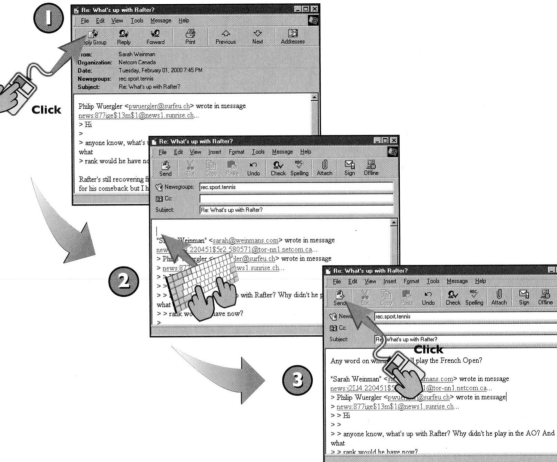

Click

Click

(1) Display the message to which you want to reply. Click the **Reply Group** button.

(2) Type your message.

(3) Click the **Send** button.

End Task

Task 12: Exiting Outlook Express

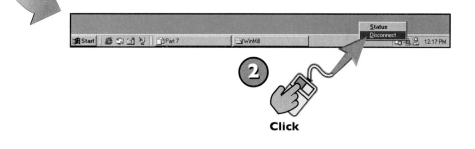

Click

Click

2

When you are finished with mail or newsgroups, you can exit Outlook Express and also log off your Internet service provider.

1 Click the **Close** button in the upper-right corner of the Outlook Express window.

2 Log off your Internet provider.

✓ **Prompted?**
You might be prompted to log off. If not, right-click the connection icon in the taskbar and select **Disconnect**.

Personalizing Windows

To make Windows more suited to how you work, Microsoft has made it easy for you to customize the program. You can move and resize the taskbar, placing it where you want on the desktop. You can adjust the colors used for onscreen elements such as the title bar. You can change how the mouse works, when sounds are played, and more. Windows Millennium includes many options for setting up your work environment just the way you want. This part shows you how to customize Windows.

Tasks

Task 1: Showing and Hiding the Taskbar

Windows's default is to show the taskbar at all times on the desktop. You can, however, hide the taskbar so that you have more room on the desktop for other windows, folders, and programs. When you hide the taskbar, it disappears while you are working in a window and then reappears when you move the mouse to the bottom of the screen.

✓ **Undo the Change**
To undo this change, use the **Start** menu to reopen the **Taskbar and Start Menu Properties** window. Click the **Auto Hide** option to remove the check mark. Then click **OK**.

✓ **Use Shortcut**
You can right-click a blank area of the taskbar and select **Properties** to make a change.

✓ **Use Small Icons**
You can also use this window to display small icons and to enable or disable the clock.

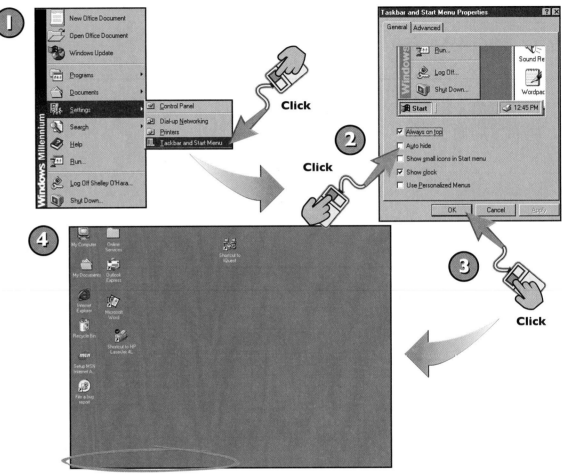

Click

Click

Click

1 Click **Start**, **Settings**, and then select **Taskbar and Start Menu**.

2 Click the **Auto hide** check box.

3 Click the **OK** button.

4 The dialog closes, and the taskbar disappears.

End Task

Task 2: Moving the Taskbar

Start Here

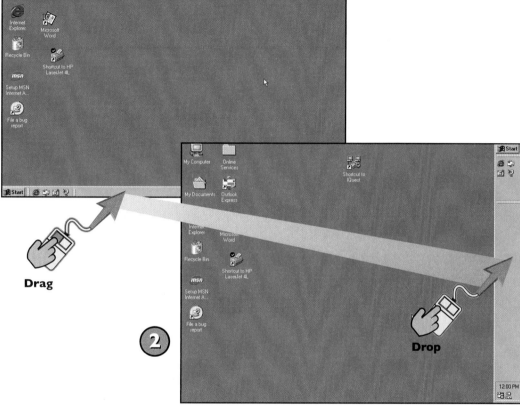

Drag

Drop

Windows enables you to place the taskbar on the top, left, right, or bottom of the screen so that the desktop is set up how you like it. Try moving the taskbar to various areas on the screen, and then choose the area you like best.

1 Position the mouse pointer anywhere on the taskbar except on a button or the clock. Press and hold the left mouse button and drag the taskbar to the location you want.

2 When you release the mouse button, the taskbar jumps to the new location.

✓ **Move Taskbar Back**
To move the taskbar back to the bottom of the screen, drag it to that area.

End Task

Task 3: Resizing the Taskbar

In addition to moving the taskbar, you can also resize it (for example, make it larger so that the buttons are bigger and easier to read). You resize the taskbar just as you resize a window—by dragging its border.

Start Here

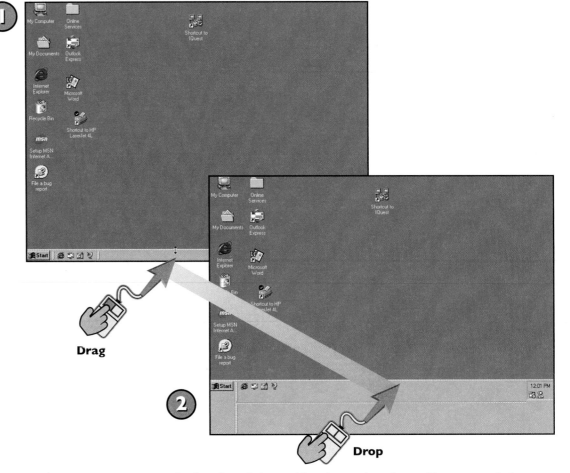

Drag

Drop

✓ **Resize Again**
Follow these same steps to resize the taskbar again. You can drag it so that it is as narrow as possible by dragging the border down until it will go no farther.

✓ **Display Other Toolbars**
You can display toolbars in the taskbar. Right-click a blank part of the taskbar and then select **Toolbars**. Check the toolbar you want to turn on.

1. Position the mouse pointer on the border of the taskbar (note that the taskbar can only be resized vertically).

2. Drag the border to resize. When you release the mouse button, the taskbar is resized.

End Task

Task 4: Personalizing the Menus

You can have Windows display just the commands you use most often. All the commands are still available, but only the most recently used commands will appear in menus. Windows will monitor the commands you use and then decide which are the frequently used commands.

① Click **Start**, **Settings**, and then select **Taskbar and Start Menu**.

② Check the **Use Personalized Menus** check box, and then click **OK**.

③ When you open a menu, you see the most frequently used commands. Notice an arrow appears at the bottom of the menu. You can display all commands by clicking the arrow.

✔️ **Show All Commands**
If you prefer to see all commands, follow these same steps, but uncheck **Use Personalized Menus**.

Task 5: Using Wallpaper for the Desktop

You can personalize your desktop in Windows by adding wallpaper. Windows offers many colorful wallpaper options, including a chateau, ocean wave, and bubbles.

Start Here

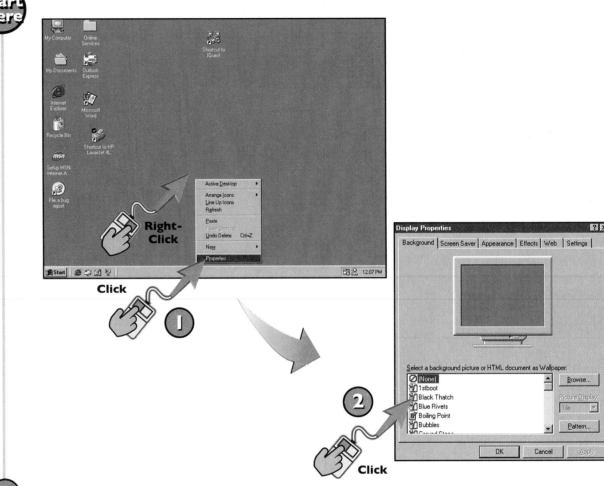

Right-Click

Click

Click

Right-click any blank area of the desktop, and then click **Properties**.

Select the wallpaper you want displayed on your desktop (use the scrollbars if necessary).

 Active Desktop
For some choices, you will be prompted to turn on Active Desktop. Click **OK**.

Next Step

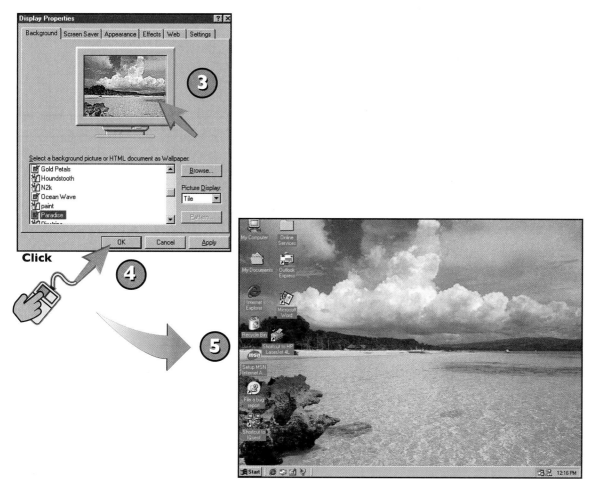

Display Properties

Background | Screen Saver | Appearance | Effects | Web | Settings

③

Click

④

⑤

Select a background picture or HTML document as Wallpaper:

- Gold Petals
- Houndstooth
- N2k
- Ocean Wave
- paint
- Paradise

Browse...

Picture Display:
Tile

Pattern...

OK | Cancel | Apply

③ The selected wallpaper appears on the sample monitor.

④ Click the **OK** button.

⑤ The wallpaper is added to your desktop background.

 Desktop Not Covered?
If you see only one small image in the center of your screen when selecting a wallpaper, click the **Picture Display** drop-down list and choose **Tile**. Click **Apply**, and then click **OK** to accept the changes.

 Turn Off Wallpaper
To revert to a plain background, follow these steps, but select **None** from the **Wallpaper** list.

End Task

Task 6: Using a Pattern for the Desktop

If you don't like the wallpaper selections, you might want to experiment with a pattern. A pattern consists of a pattern of dots repeated in the screen colors. Wallpaper is an image that can have different colors. Windows offers paisley, tulip, waffle, and box background patterns (among others).

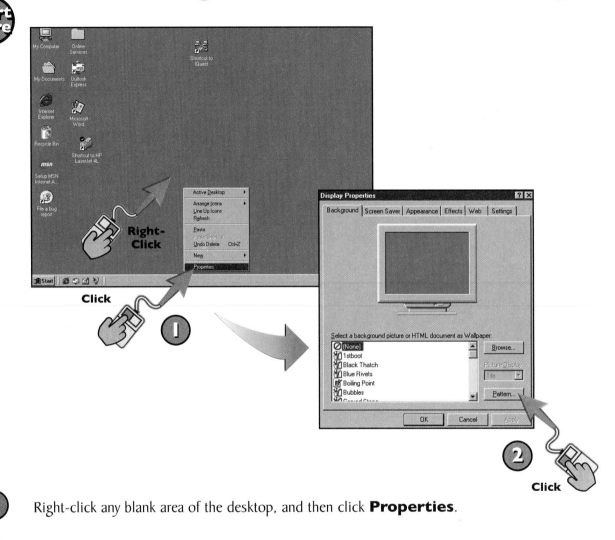

1 Right-click any blank area of the desktop, and then click **Properties**.

2 Click the **Pattern** button.

Next Step

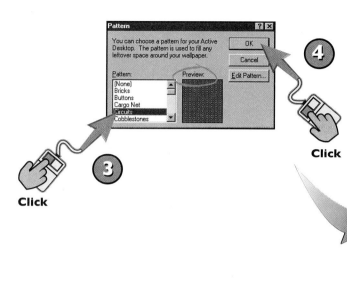

Click

Click

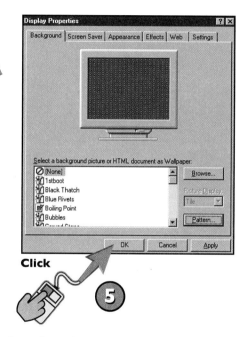

Click

3 Select the pattern you want displayed on your desktop. The selected pattern appears in the **Preview** area.

4 Click the **OK** button to use this pattern and to close the **Pattern** dialog box.

5 You see the sample in the **Display Properties** dialog box. Click **OK**. Windows uses the selected pattern on your desktop.

✅ **Computer Slow?**
Using wallpaper and patterns generally slows the speed of your computer and taxes its memory. If your applications seem too slow or if you decide you don't want a pattern or wallpaper, return to the **Display Properties** dialog box, click the **Patterns** button, and choose **(None)**.

✅ **Wallpaper or Pattern**
You cannot use both a wallpaper and a pattern. If you select a wallpaper, the **Pattern** button is dimmed. If you want to use a pattern, select **(None)** from the **Wallpaper** list.

End Task

Task 7: Changing the Colors Windows Uses

Windows enables you to change the sets of colors used for certain onscreen elements such as the title bar, background, and so on. These sets of colors are called *schemes*, and you can select colors that work best for you and your monitor. Lighter colors might, for example, make working in some Windows applications easier on your eyes. On the other hand, you might prefer bright and lively colors.

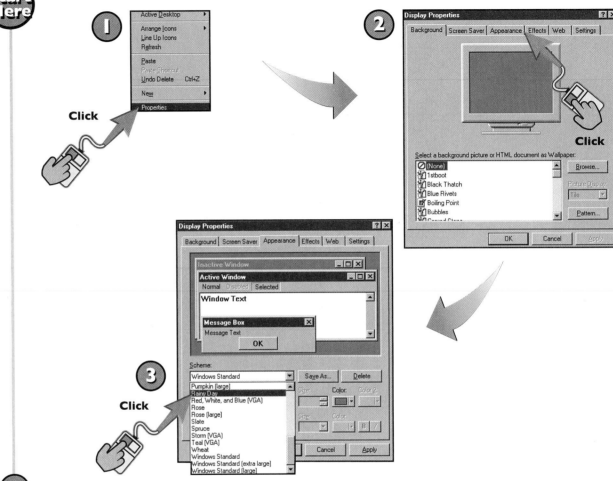

Click

Click

Click

① Right-click any blank area of the desktop, and then click **Properties**.

② Click the **Appearance** tab.

③ From the **Scheme** drop-down list, select any of the available schemes.

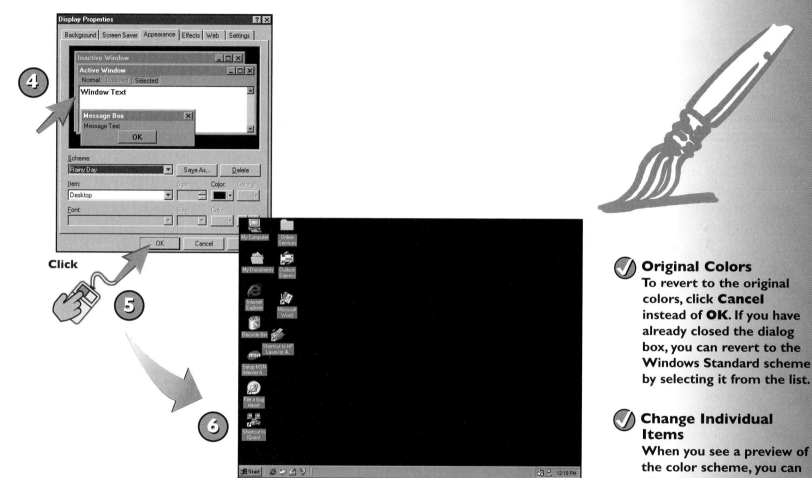

Click

Original Colors
To revert to the original colors, click **Cancel** instead of **OK**. If you have already closed the dialog box, you can revert to the Windows Standard scheme by selecting it from the list.

Change Individual Items
When you see a preview of the color scheme, you can change any individual item's color by clicking the item, and then selecting a different color from the **Color** list at the bottom of the window. When you're satisfied with your changes, click **OK** to accept the changes.

④ The color scheme you selected (in this case, **Rainy Day**) appears in the sample box.

⑤ Click the **OK** button to accept the changes.

⑥ Windows uses the new set of colors you selected.

Task 8: Using a Screen Saver

In the past, when you used Windows or Windows applications, the concentration of bright or white colors on older monitors would, over time, burn into the screen (commonly called "burn in"). When this happened, you saw a "ghost" of the Windows screen on your display after you turned off your computer. A screen saver (a moving pattern of dark and light colors or images) helped protect your screen from burn in by displaying a pattern whenever the computer was on but inactive. Even though modern monitors do not suffer from burn in, many still use screen savers for fun.

✓ **Set Screen Saver Options**
Click the **Settings** button to select options for how the screen saver is displayed; these options vary depending on the screen saver. Make your choices and click the **OK** button.

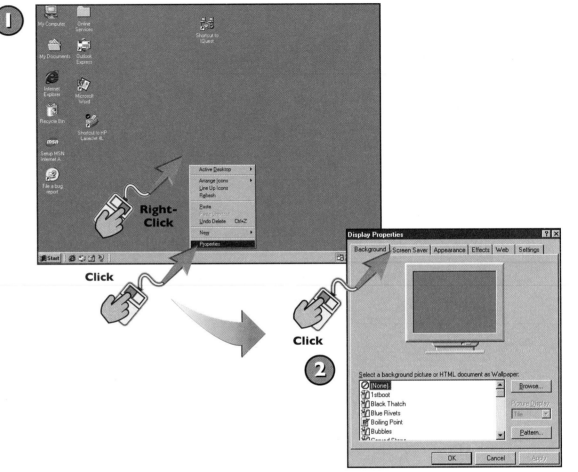

1 Right-click any blank area of the desktop, and then click **Properties**.

2 Click the **Screen Saver** tab.

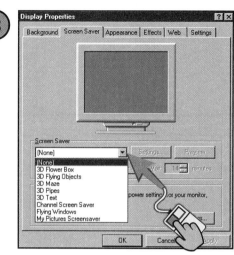

Click

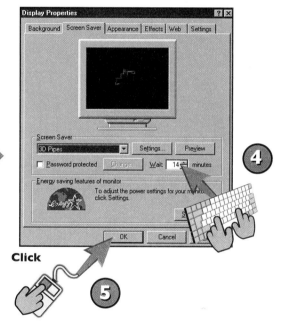

Click

③ Click the **Screen Saver** drop-down list box arrow to display the list of available screen savers, and then select the screen saver you want to use.

④ The selected screen saver appears on the sample monitor. If you want to use it, type in the **Wait** text box the number of minutes you want Windows to wait before it starts the screen saver.

⑤ Click the **OK** button.

✓ **Preview Screen Saver**
If you want to see what the screen saver will look like when it is displayed on the full screen, click the **Preview** button to direct Windows to display the saver on the entire screen. Click the mouse button or press the spacebar to return to the **Display Properties** dialog box.

✓ **Deactivate Screen Saver**
When the screen saver is displayed, move the mouse or press the spacebar to return to the normal view.

✓ **Turn Off Screen Saver**
To turn off the screen saver, invoke the **Display Properties** dialog box, click the **Screen Saver** tab, and select **None**. Click the **OK** button.

Task 9: Changing How Your Monitor Works

Many monitors enable you to select certain options about how they operate, such as the number of colors they display or their resolution. (Resolution measures the number of pixels or picture elements displayed. An example of a common resolution is 800×600.) In most cases, changing these options is not necessary. However, if you get a new monitor, want to update your monitor driver, or want to change how the monitor looks you might need to change its display properties.

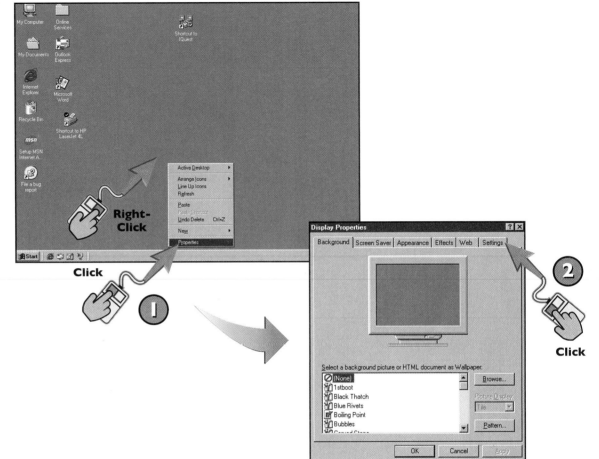

Right-Click

Click

Click

Start Here

①

②

① Right-click any blank area of the desktop, and then click **Properties**.

Choices Vary
The available choices will depend on your monitor. If the settings you select don't look right, revert to the original ones.

② Click the **Settings** tab.

Next Step

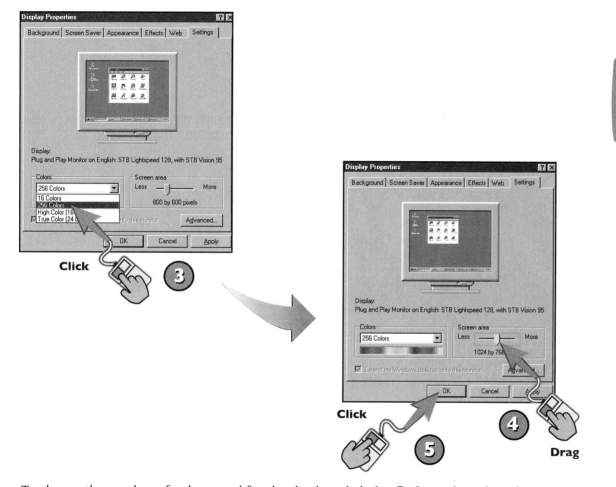

Click

Click

Drag

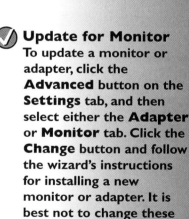

Update for Monitor
To update a monitor or adapter, click the **Advanced** button on the **Settings** tab, and then select either the **Adapter** or **Monitor** tab. Click the **Change** button and follow the wizard's instructions for installing a new monitor or adapter. It is best not to change these setting unless you have to.

No Risk
Windows will not let you choose an invalid screen resolution or number of colors, so you can play around with those settings until you're happy with the results.

3 To change the number of colors used for the display, click the **Colors** drop-down list and choose the number you want.

4 To change the resolution, drag the **Screen area** bar to the desired setting.

5 Click the **OK** button.

Another way to experiment with the appearance of the desktop is to change how the icons are displayed. You can select a different picture for any of the default icons. Windows Millennium comes with several icons to choose from. You can also select the size and colors used for icons on the desktop.

Task 10: Changing How the Desktop Icons Look

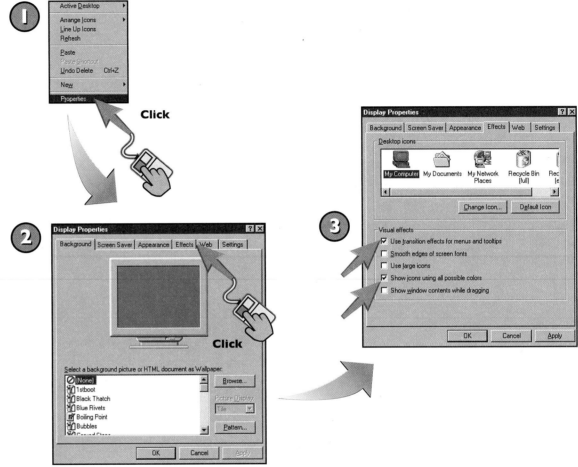

Click

Click

1. Right-click any blank area of the desktop, and then click **Properties**.

2. Click the **Effects** tab.

3. Select the visual effects you want in the **Visual effects** section. A check mark next to an option indicates that the option is active. If an option is unchecked, it is inactive.

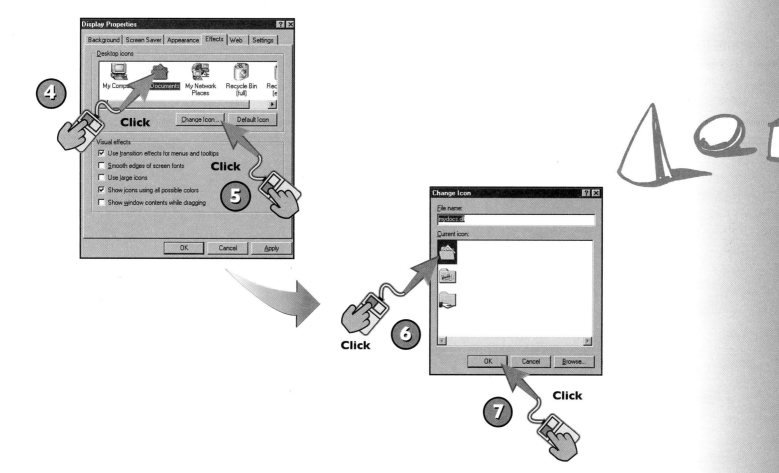

4 To use a different icon, select the icon you want to change.

5 Click the **Change Icon** button.

6 Select the icon you want to use instead.

7 Click the **OK** button in the **Change Icon** dialog box, and then click the **OK** button to close the **Display Properties** dialog box.

 Use Original Icons
To go back to the original icon, display the **Effects** tab and select the icon. Click the **Default Icon** button, and then click the **OK** button.

 End Task

Task 11: Using Active Desktop

If you have an Internet connection and want fast access to Internet content, you can turn on Windows's Active Desktop. When this feature is on, you can display and access Web channels and your home page. (For more information about browsing the Internet, see Part 7, "Connecting to Online Services and the Internet.")

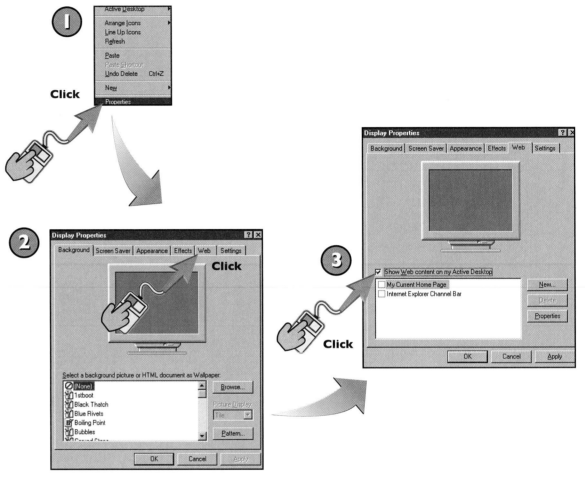

Click

Click

Click

1. Right-click any blank area of the desktop, and then click **Properties**.

2. Click the **Web** tab.

3. Check the **Show Web content on my Active Desktop** check box to enable this feature.

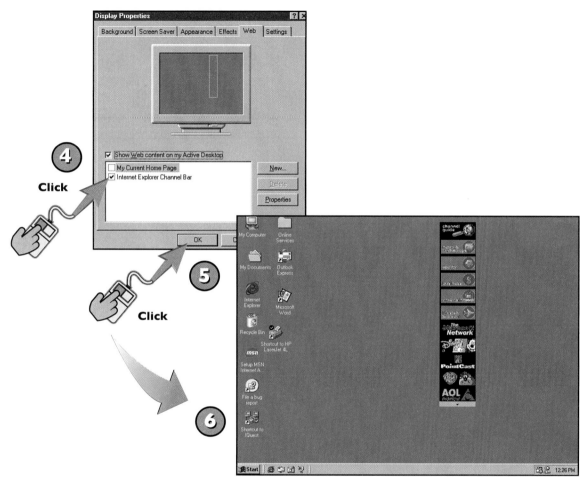

Click

Click

4 To display the channel bar, check the **Internet Explorer Channel Bar** check box.

5 Click the **OK** button.

6 The desktop displays with Internet content.

✅ **Turn Off Active Desktop**
To revert to the regular desktop, right-click a blank area of the desktop, choose **Active Desktop**, and click **Show Web Content** to deselect this option.

✅ **Single-Click Icons**
To single-click folders and icons, change the folder options. Refer to Part 2, "Working with Disks, Folders, and Files," for more information.

Task 12: Working with Channels

You can display channels on your desktop and then access those Web sites. You can select from several channels, including Disney, Warner Bros., MSNBC, and others. (For more information about browsing the Internet, see Part 7, "Connecting to Online Services and the Internet.")

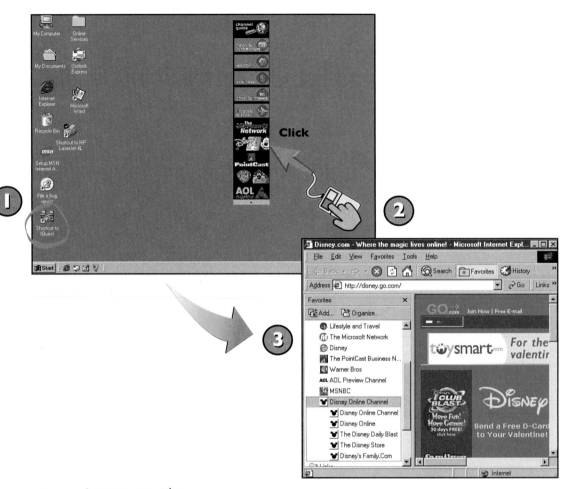

✓ **Hide the Channel Bar**
To hide the channel bar, right-click a blank area of the desktop, choose **Active Desktop**, and then uncheck **Internet Explorer Channel Bar**.

✓ **Get Connected**
You might be able to view some canned content without being connected, but you must be connected to view new content.

1 Log on to your Internet provider.

2 To view a channel, click it in the channel bar.

3 Windows starts Internet Explorer and displays that site.

Task 13: Viewing Your Home Page on Your Desktop

In addition to channels, you can also display your Internet home page on the desktop. You can then access any of these features right from the Windows desktop.

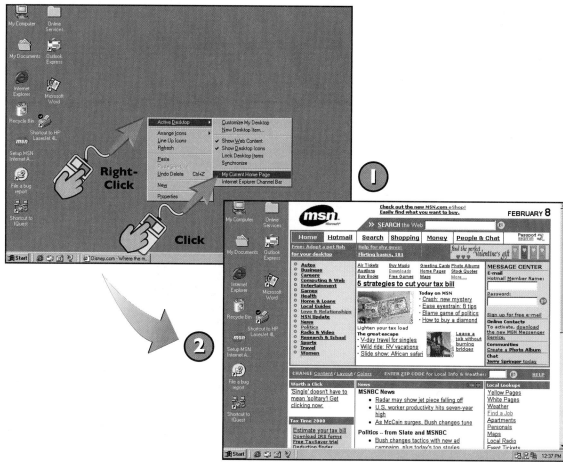

Right-Click

Click

Use Links
If you are connected to the Internet, you can click any link on your home page to go to that site.

Resize Home Page
You can resize the home page object on the desktop using the buttons in the title bar (minimize, maximize, and restore). You can also drag the border to change the size.

(1) Right-click the desktop, select **Active Desktop**, and then check **My Current Home Page**.

(2) Your home page is displayed as Web content on the desktop.

Task 14: Adding Web Content to the Desktop

Start Here

In addition to channels and your home page, you can add links to other Web sites to the desktop. You can then access this site with a click of the mouse. To add Web content, you must know the address of the site. (For more information on Web browsing, see Part 7, "Connecting to Online Services and the Internet.")

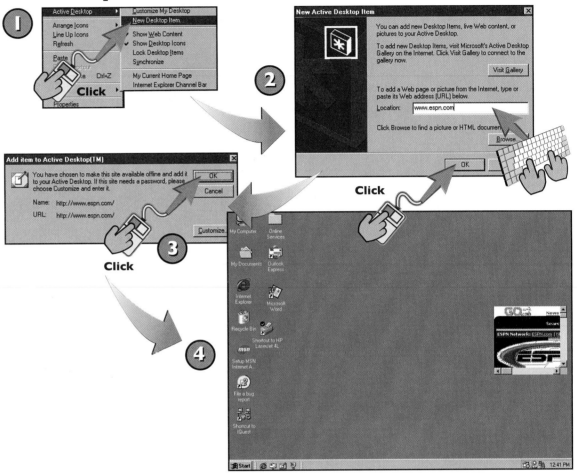

Click

Click

Click

 Resize Content
To resize the content, drag one of its borders.

 Turn Off
To turn off the Web desktop item, right-click the desktop, select **Active Desktop**, and then uncheck the item you've added. (The name will vary depending on the site you've added.)

1. Right-click the desktop, select **Active Desktop**, and then select **New Desktop Item**.

2. Type the location of the site, and then click **OK**.

3. Click **OK** when you see a message about offline viewing. The content is downloaded and synchronized.

4. The site content is displayed on your desktop.

End Task

Task 15: Changing the System Date and Time

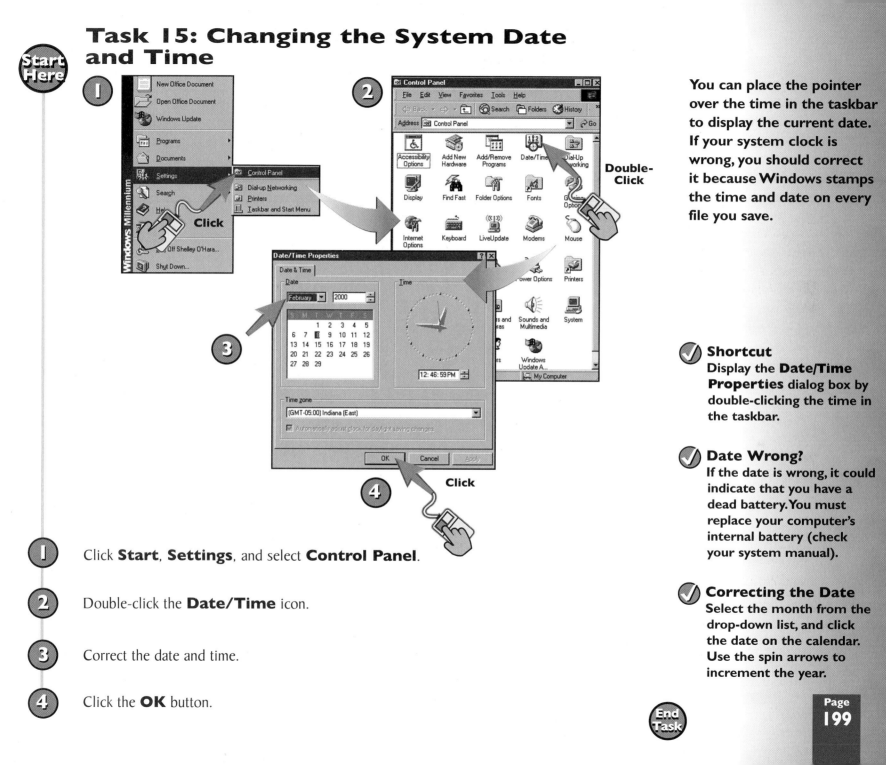

Start Here

You can place the pointer over the time in the taskbar to display the current date. If your system clock is wrong, you should correct it because Windows stamps the time and date on every file you save.

✅ **Shortcut**
Display the **Date/Time Properties** dialog box by double-clicking the time in the taskbar.

✅ **Date Wrong?**
If the date is wrong, it could indicate that you have a dead battery. You must replace your computer's internal battery (check your system manual).

✅ **Correcting the Date**
Select the month from the drop-down list, and click the date on the calendar. Use the spin arrows to increment the year.

1 Click **Start**, **Settings**, and select **Control Panel**.

2 Double-click the **Date/Time** icon.

3 Correct the date and time.

4 Click the **OK** button.

End Task

Task 16: Changing How the Mouse Works

You can adjust the mouse buttons and double-click speed to make using the mouse more comfortable for you. Suppose, for example, that you are left-handed; switching the left and right mouse buttons can make your work much easier. Likewise, if you are having trouble getting the double-click right, you can change the double-click speed on the mouse. You can also slow your pointer speed down so that you can easily find your mouse onscreen when you move it quickly.

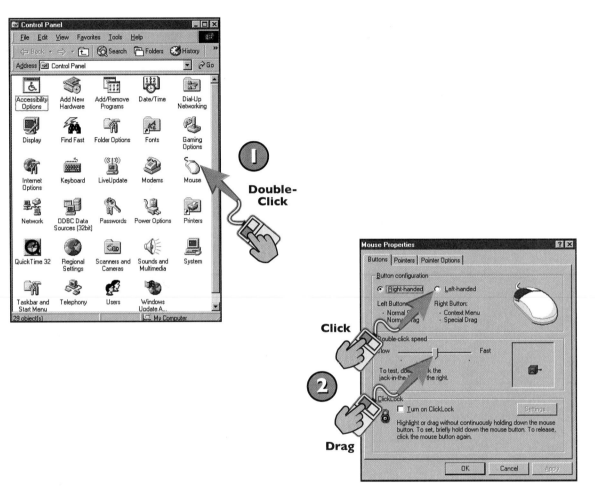

Start Here

Double-Click

Click

Drag

① Double-click the **Mouse** icon in the Control Panel (refer to Task 15 if you need help opening the Control Panel).

② If you want to switch the mouse buttons, select the **Left-handed** radio button. To change the double-click speed, drag the **Double-click speed** lever between **Slow** and **Fast**.

Next Step

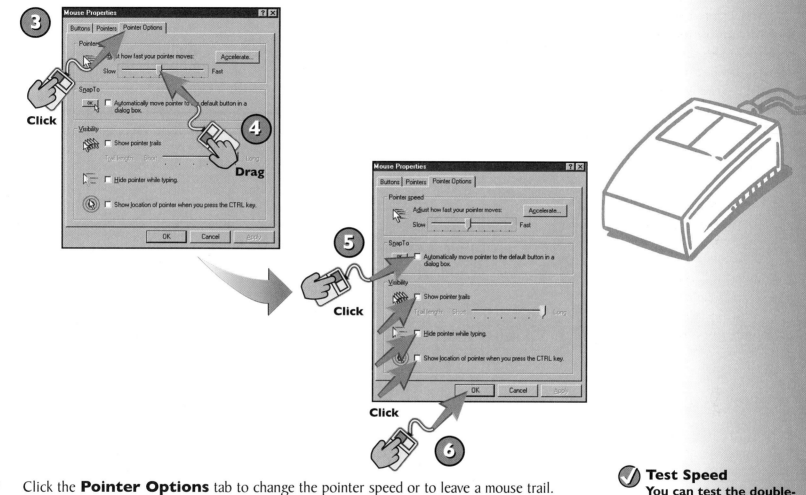

Click

Drag

Click

Click

---

③ Click the **Pointer Options** tab to change the pointer speed or to leave a mouse trail.

④ Adjust the pointer speed by dragging the **Pointer speed** lever between **Slow** and **Fast**.

⑤ Click the check box in the **SnapTo** area to snap to the default button.

⑥ Make any changes to the pointer options in the **Visibility** area and then click the **OK** button.

Test Speed
You can test the double-click speed by double-clicking in the **Test** box. When you double-click correctly, a Jack-in-the-box pops out. Double-click again, and Jack goes back into the box.

Task 17: Changing How the Mouse Pointers Look

You can change the way the mouse pointer appears onscreen. Depending on the action, the pointer takes several different shapes. For example, when Windows is busy, you see an hourglass. You can select a different set of shapes (called a scheme) if you prefer.

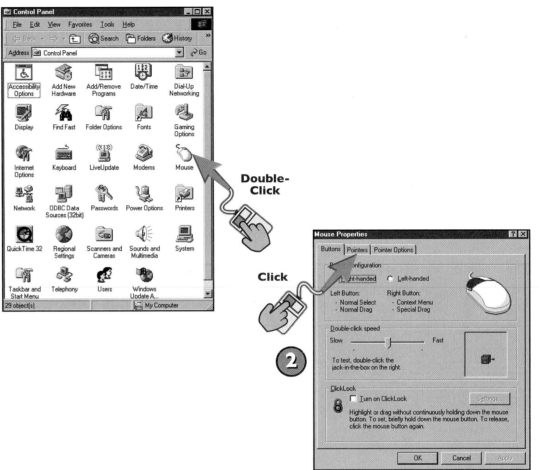

Double-Click

Click

Double-click the **Mouse** icon in the Control Panel (refer to Task 15 if you need help opening the Control Panel).

Click the **Pointers** tab.

Next Step

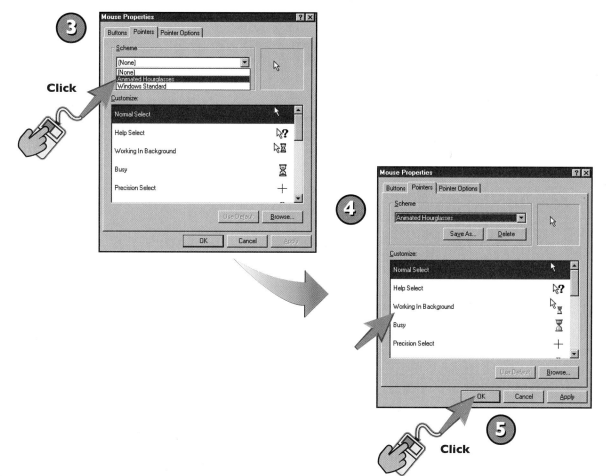

Click

Click

3 Display the **Scheme** drop-down list and choose the scheme you want to use.

4 A preview of each pointer in the chosen scheme (in this case, **Animated Hourglasses**) is displayed.

5 Click **OK** to accept the changes and to close the dialog box.

✓ **Use Original Pointers**
To go back to the default scheme, display the **Pointers** tab of the **Mouse Properties** dialog box, and then select **None** from the **Scheme** drop-down list.

✓ **Set Individual Pointers**
You can select which pointer to use for each individual action. Simply select the action you want to change, click the **Browse** button, select the pointer you want to use, and click **Open**. Do this for each action you want to change, and then click the **OK** button.

End Task

Task 18: Playing Sounds for Certain Windows Actions

When you perform certain actions in Windows Millennium, you might hear a sound. For example, you hear a sound when Windows Millennium is started. You might hear a sound when an alert box is displayed. You can stick with the default sounds, or you can select a different sound to use for each key Windows event.

 Start Here

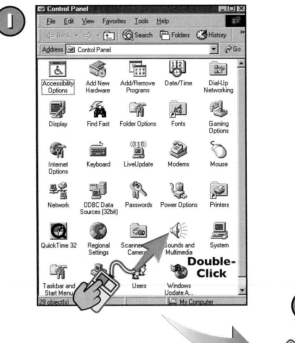

Double-Click

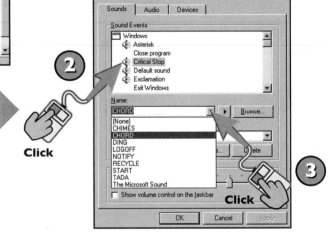

Click

Click

 **Select a Scheme**
If you have sound schemes, you can select a set of sounds by displaying the **Schemes** drop-down list in the **Sound Properties** dialog box. Select the scheme you want, and then click **OK**.

1 Double-click the **Sounds and Multimedia** icon in the Control Panel (refer to Task 15 if you need help opening the Control Panel).

2 Select the sound event you want to change.

3 Display the **Name** drop-down list to select the sound that you want to assign to that event.

 Next Step

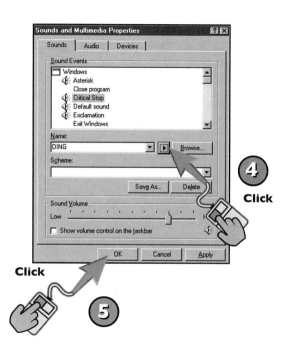

Click

Click

To hear a preview of the sound, click the **Play** button.

Click **OK** to accept the changes and to close the dialog box.

✓ **No Sound?**
If you don't want a sound played for an event, select that event and choose **None** from the **Name** list.

✓ **Set Audio Devices**
You can click the **Audio** tab and select the devices used for sound playback, sound recording, and MIDI music playback.

Task 19: Setting Up Windows for Multiple Users

If more than one person uses your PC, you might want to personalize certain Windows settings for each person. For example, you can customize the desktop, **Start** menu, **Favorites** folder, **My Documents** folder, and more. Each person can set up Windows the way he or she wants and then create a user profile. Each time that person logs on, all those settings will be used.

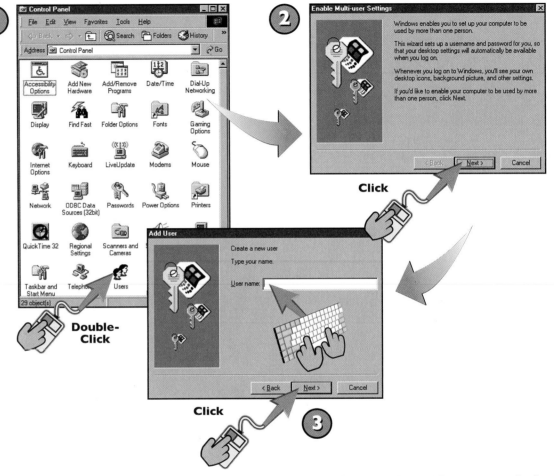

Double-Click

Click

Click

(1) Double-click the **Users** icon in the Control Panel to start the **Multiple Users** wizard. If you need help opening the Control Panel, refer to Task 15.

(2) Click the **Next** button.

(3) Type the name of the person you are setting up, and then click **Next**.

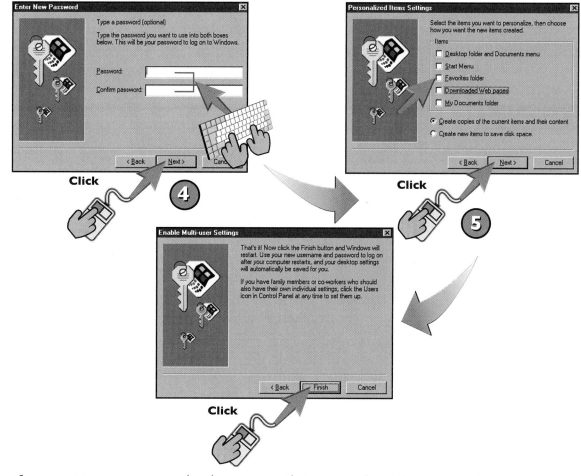

Click

Click

Click

4 If you want to use a password to log on, type that password and then confirm the password by typing it again. After you finish, click **Next**.

5 From the **Items** section, select the items you want to save in this profile. After you finish, click **Next**.

6 Click the **Finish** button. Windows will restart, and you will be prompted to type your user name and password to log on.

All Users
Follow this procedure to set up profiles for each user.

Cancel Changes
Any changes you make in this dialog box can easily be reversed. Simply choose **Cancel** to close the dialog box.

Task 20: Setting Up Windows for the Impaired

You can employ certain features of Windows Millennium to make it easier to use. You can select different settings for the keyboard, sounds, display, and mouse.

Start Here

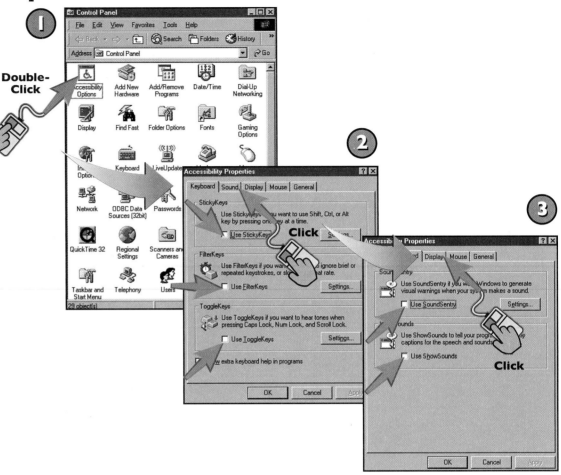

Double-Click

---

1 Double-click the **Accessibility Options** icon in the Control Panel. If you need help reaching the Control Panel, refer to Task 15.

2 Enable any keyboard features by checking the appropriate check box. After you finish, click the **Sound** tab.

3 Select to display visual warnings and/or captions for alert messages, and then click the **Display** tab.

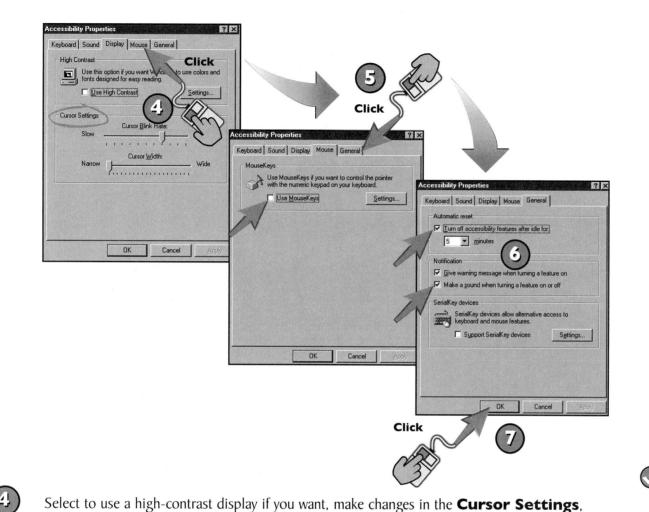

Click

Click

Click

4 Select to use a high-contrast display if you want, make changes in the **Cursor Settings**, and then click the **Mouse** tab.

5 Select to use the numeric keypad to control the mouse, and then click the **General** tab.

6 Make changes as needed to the **Automatic reset** and **Notification** options.

7 Click the **OK** button.

✅ **Key Options**
You can use StickyKeys to press one key at a time for key combinations. Use FilterKeys to ignore brief repeated keystrokes. Use ToggleKeys to play a tone when you have pressed Caps Lock, Num Lock, or Scroll Lock.

End Task

Task 21: Setting Power Options

To conserve power, you can elect to use a power scheme. If you do not use your PC within the timeframe you select, Windows will turn off the monitor and hard disk. You can also select to put the system on standby.

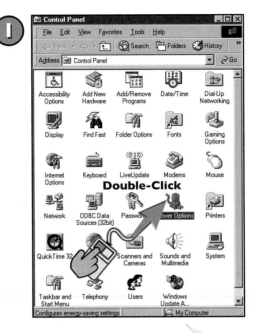

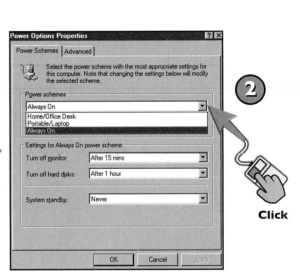

Click

① Double-click the **Power Options** icon in the Control Panel. If you need help opening the Control Panel, refer to Task 15.

② To select a preset scheme, display the **Power schemes** drop-down list and select a scheme.

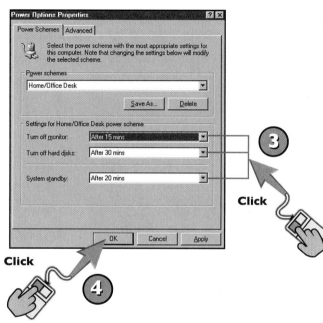

Click

Click

③ To change the time settings, display the drop-down list and select the time interval for when to turn off the monitor, when to turn off the hard disks, and when to go on system standby.

④ Click **OK**.

✅ **Deactivate Standby**
If your computer goes on standby, you can reactivate it by pressing a few keys on the keyboard.

PART 10

Setting Up Programs

Most of the time you spend using your computer will be spent using some type of application. To make it as easy as possible, Windows Millennium enables you to set up several ways to start programs. You can create shortcuts to a program and place the shortcut on the desktop to make it more accessible. You can rearrange the programs on the **Start** menu so that they are more suited to how you work. You can install new programs and remove programs you no longer use. There is no right or wrong way to set up your programs; you can select the style and organization that most suit you.

Tasks

Task 1: Adding Shortcuts

You can create shortcuts and place them on the desktop to provide quick access to programs. You can then double-click a shortcut to quickly start that program—without having to open menus and folders.

① Display the program file for which you want to create a shortcut icon.

② Holding down your right mouse button, drag the program file from the window to your desktop.

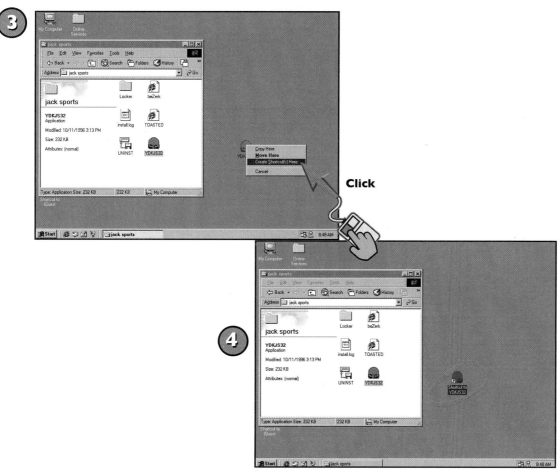

Click

Shortcut to File or Printer
You can create shortcut icons to files or folders (covered in Part 2, "Working with Disks, Folders, and Files") or to your printer (covered in Part 4, "Printing with Windows").

Search for a File
If you can't find the program file, try searching for it. Finding a particular file is covered in Part 3, "Using Applications in Windows Millennium."

3 Release the button, and then choose **Create Shortcut(s) Here** from the ensuing shortcut menu.

4 Windows adds the shortcut to your desktop.

Task 2: Renaming Shortcuts

When you create a
shortcut, Windows
Millennium assigns a name
to the icon, but you might
want to use a different
name. For example, you
might prefer the name
Word rather than
WinWord. You can rename
any shortcut icon on your
desktop.

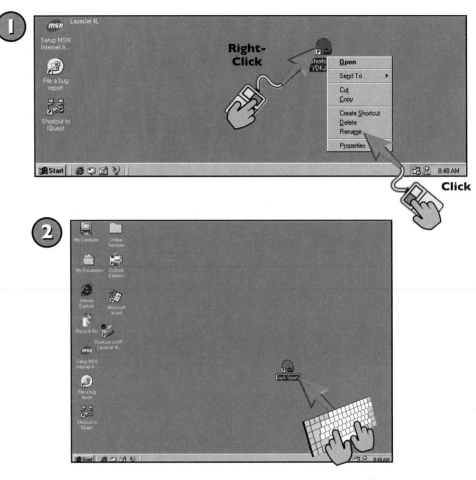

Right-click the selected icon, and then click the **Rename** command.

Type the new shortcut name, and press **Enter**.

Task 3: Deleting Shortcuts

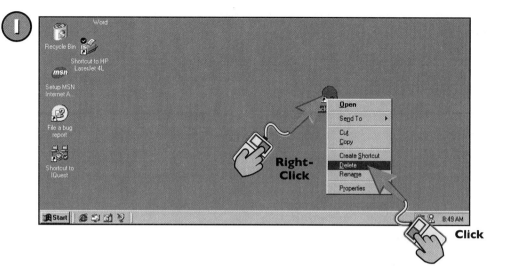

You can use shortcuts to quickly open the program you need. But as time passes, your needs for programs might change, and the desktop might become cluttered with program icons you no longer need. Just as you can create new shortcuts as you add new programs, you can delete shortcuts you no longer use.

Right-click the selected icon, and click the **Delete** command.

In the **Confirm Shortcut Delete** dialog box, click **Yes** to delete the shortcut.

What Happens When You Delete?

Deleting a shortcut does not delete that program from your hard drive. To delete the program, you must uninstall it or delete the program and its related folders and files. Note that you can do so using the **Add/Remove Programs** link at the bottom of the dialog box.

Task 4: Adding Programs to the Start Menu

When you install most programs, they are added automatically to the **Start** menu. If a program is not added during installation, you can add it yourself.

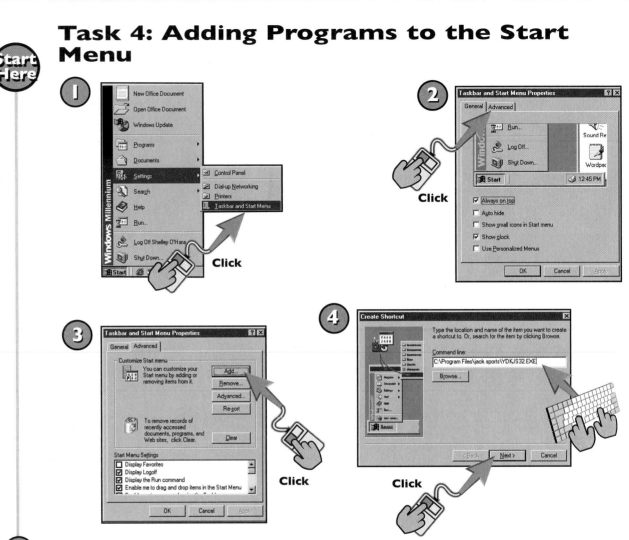

Start Here

Click

Click

Click

Click

Click

✓ **Use the Browse Button**
If you don't know the command line, click the **Browse** button, and then select the folder and the program name from the **Browse** dialog box.

1 Click **Start**, **Settings**, and then click **Taskbar and Start Menu**.

2 Click the **Advanced** tab.

3 Click the **Add** button.

4 Enter the command line for the program you want to add, and then click the **Next** button.

Next Step

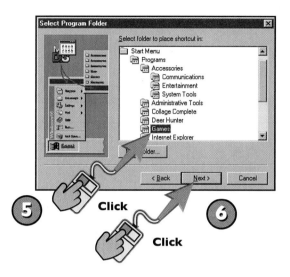

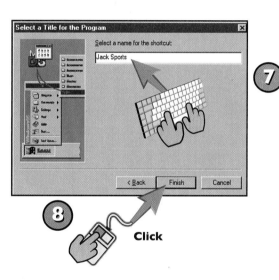

Click

Click

Click

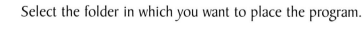

Close the Dialog Box
To close the **Taskbar and Start Menu Properties** dialog box after adding the program, click **OK**.

Add New Folder
You can click the **New Folder** button to add a new folder (also see Task 6, "Adding Folders to the Start Menu").

Remove a Program
To remove a program from the **Start** menu, see Task 5, "Deleting Programs from the Start Menu."

(5) Select the folder in which you want to place the program.

(6) Click the **Next** button.

(7) Enter a name in the text box or accept the one Windows displays.

(8) Click the **Finish** button to add the new program.

End Task

Page
219

Task 5: Deleting Programs from the Start Menu

If your **Start** menu becomes cluttered, you might want to delete icons for programs that you don't use. At first, you might go a little crazy and add all kinds of icons. But after you use the computer more and more, you might want to streamline the **Start** menu and weed out programs that you don't use.

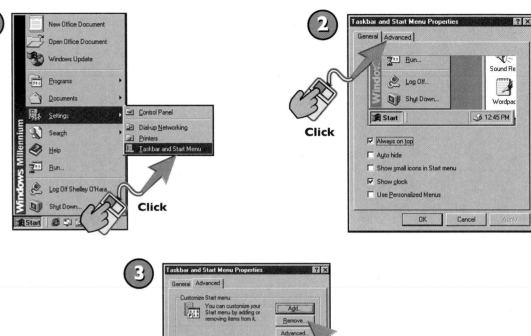

Click **Start**, **Settings**, and then click the **Taskbar and Start Menu** command.

Click the **Advanced** tab.

Click the **Remove** button.

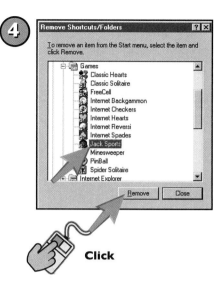

Click

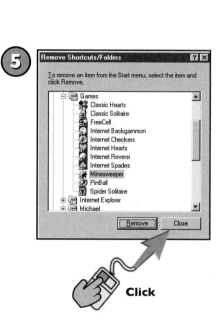

Click

✔️ **Remove a Folder**
You can follow this procedure to remove a folder from the **Start** menu. Simply select the folder, and then click the **Remove** button. You are prompted to confirm the removal; click **Yes**. The folder and all its contents are removed.

⚠️ **WARNING!**
Keep in mind that removing a program from the **Start** menu does not remove the program and its files from your hard disk. To do this, you must uninstall the program or manually delete it and its related folders and files. See Task 10, "Uninstalling Applications."

4 Select the program you want to remove, and then click the **Remove** button.

5 The program is removed. Click the **Close** button to close this dialog box. Then click **OK** to close the **Taskbar and Start Menu Properties** dialog box.

✔️ **Expand the Listing**
To display and select the program you want to remove, you might need to expand the folder listings. Click the plus sign next to the folder that contains the desired program.

Task 6: Adding Folders to the Start Menu

When you install a new program, that program's installation sets up program folders and icons for itself. If you don't like the arrangement of the folders and icons, you can change it. For example, if more than one person uses your PC, you might set up folders for each person and then add the programs that a certain person uses to his or her folder.

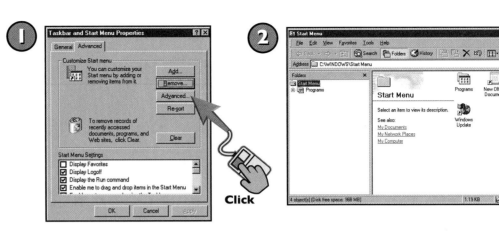

Start Here

Click

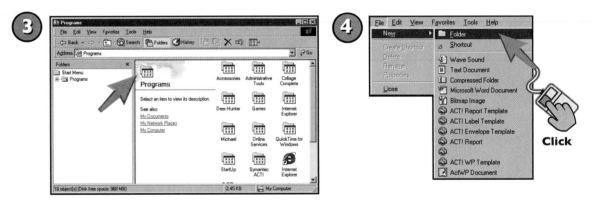

Click

1. Click the **Advanced** button on the **Advanced** tab. Refer to Task 5 if you need help reaching this tab.

2. The **Start** menu is displayed in a folder window with the folder list on the left and the **Start Menu** folder on the right.

3. Open the folder in which the new folder should be placed. For this example, I'm placing the new folder within the **Programs** folder, so I've opened **Programs**.

4. Click **File**, select **New**, and then click **Folder**.

Next Step

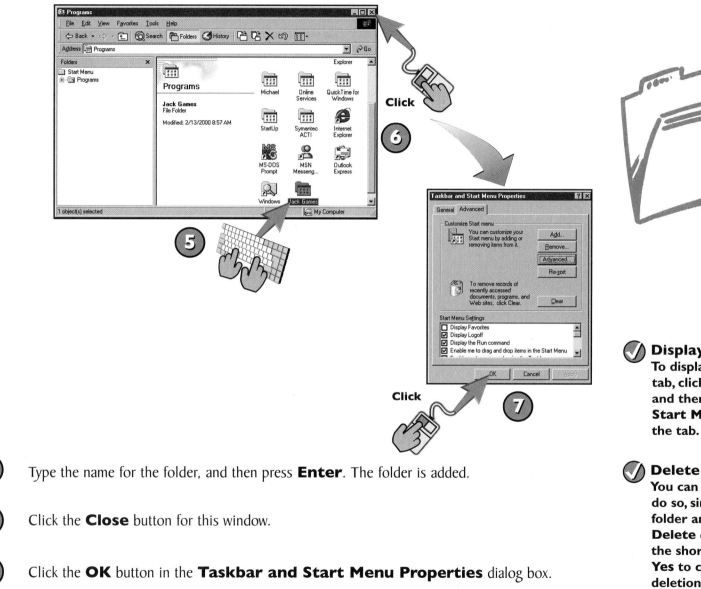

Click

Click

6

5

7

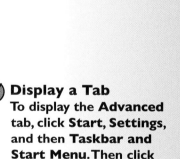

✅ **Display a Tab**
To display the **Advanced** tab, click **Start, Settings,** and then **Taskbar and Start Menu.** Then click the tab.

5 Type the name for the folder, and then press **Enter**. The folder is added.

6 Click the **Close** button for this window.

✅ **Delete Folders**
You can delete folders. To do so, simply right-click the folder and select the **Delete** command from the shortcut menu. Click **Yes** to confirm the deletion.

7 Click the **OK** button in the **Taskbar and Start Menu Properties** dialog box.

End Task

Task 7: Rearranging the Start Menu

After you set up folders, you can organize your **Start** menu, putting the program icons in the folder and order you want.

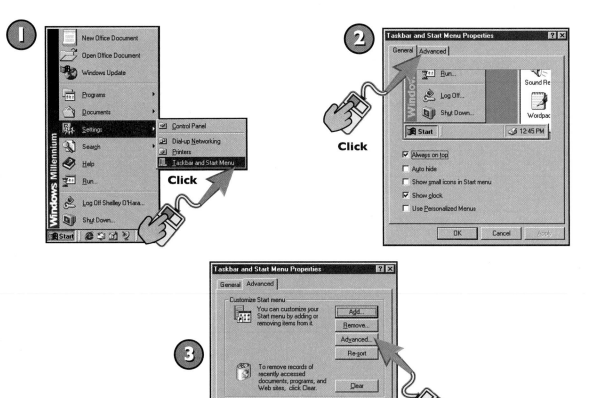

Click

Click

Click

Click

 Click **Start**, **Settings**, and then click the **Taskbar and Start Menu** command.

Click the **Advanced** tab.

Click the **Advanced** button.

Next Step

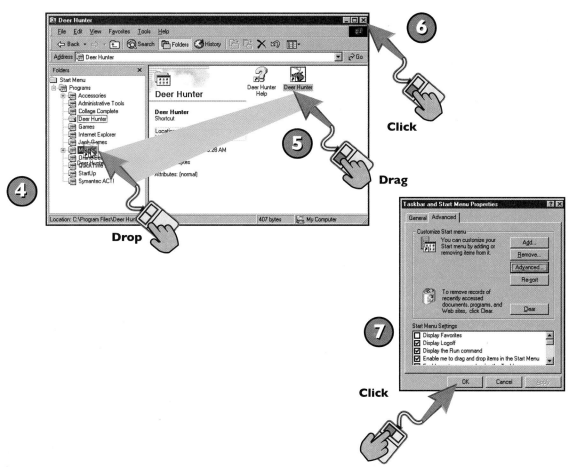

Click

Drag

Drop

Click

<table>
<tr><td>④</td><td>In the left pane, expand the folder listing until you see the folder where you want to place the program.</td></tr>
<tr><td>⑤</td><td>In the right pane, open the folder than contains the program. Drag the program icon from the right pane to the folder in the left pane.</td></tr>
<tr><td>⑥</td><td>Click the **Close** button for the window.</td></tr>
<tr><td>⑦</td><td>Click the **OK** button in the **Taskbar and Start Menu Properties** dialog box.</td></tr>
</table>

✅ **Re-Sort**
You can go back to the default order of the folders and icons by clicking the **Re-sort** button in the **Taskbar and Start Menu Properties** dialog box.

Windows enables you to start one or more programs at the same time that you start Windows by turning your computer on. Applications you might want to open automatically include those that you use every day or those that you use first thing every morning.

Task 8: Starting an Application When You Start Windows

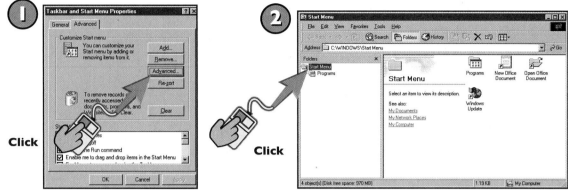

Click

Click

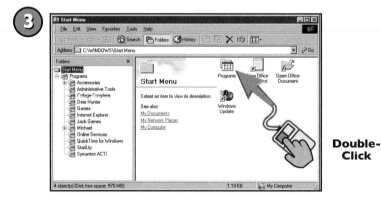

Double-Click

 **Expand the List**
If necessary, expand the **Programs** list to display the **StartUp** folder.

1 In the **Advanced** tab of the **Taskbar and Start Menu Properties** dialog box, click the **Advanced** button (see Task 5 to learn about opening this dialog box).

2 You see a folder window with the folder list displayed. Click the **+** sign next to the **Programs** folder.

3 You see the **StartUp** folder listed. In the pane on the right, open the folder that contains the program you want to add to this folder.

Next Step

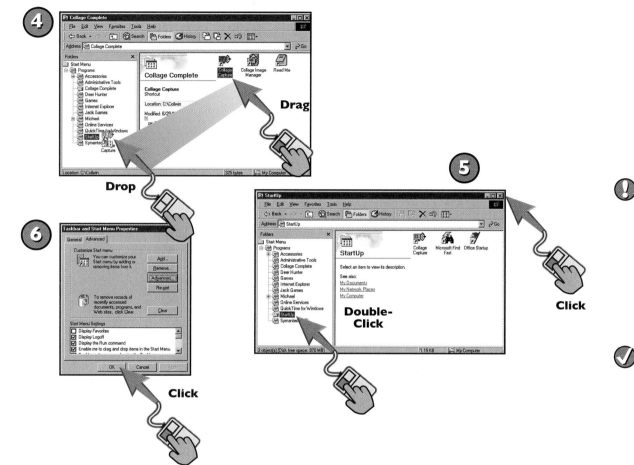

Select the icon for the program (in this case, **Collage Capture**). Hold down the **Ctrl** key and drag the icon to the **StartUp** folder.

You can double-click the **StartUp** folder to check the icon. Then click the **Close** (×) button for this window.

Click the **OK** button in the **Taskbar and Start Menu Properties** dialog box.

WARNING!
If you don't turn off your computer each night and then turn it on again when you begin work, these programs will not start each morning. They are started only when you start Windows.

Remove a Program
To remove an icon from the **StartUp** window, click the **Remove** button in the **Advanced** tab of the **Taskbar and Start Menu Properties** dialog box to display the **Remove Shortcuts/Folders** dialog box. Then choose the item you want to remove from the menu and click the **Remove** button. Close the **Remove Shortcuts/ Folders** dialog box, and then click **OK**.

Task 9: Installing Applications

Start Here

When you bought your computer, it might have come with certain programs already installed. If you want to add to these, you can purchase additional programs and then add them to your system. Installing a new program basically copies the program files to a folder on your system, and then adds a program icon for starting that program. The program's installation might also make changes to other files or programs on your system.

✅ **Use the Run Command**

If this procedure does not work, you can use the **Run** command to run the installation program. Insert the CD-ROM or disk into the appropriate drive, and then click the **Start** button and choose **Run**. Enter the disk drive and command for the installation program, and click **OK**. Follow the onscreen instructions.

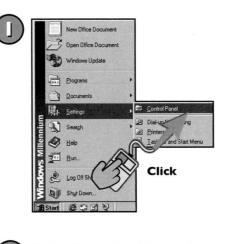

Click

Double-Click

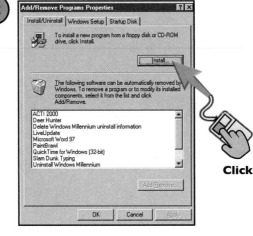

Click

1️⃣ Click **Start**, **Settings**, and click **Control Panel**.

2️⃣ Double-click the **Add/Remove Programs** icon.

3️⃣ Click the **Install** button.

Next Step

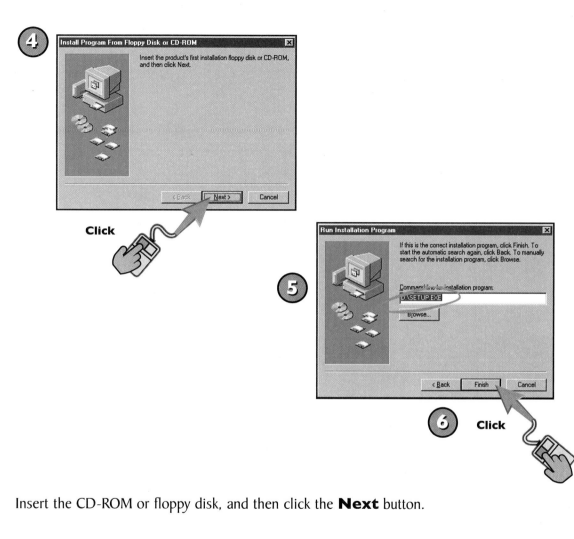

Click

Click

✓ **Uninstall a Program**
For help on uninstalling applications, see Task 10, "Uninstalling Applications."

✓ **Adding Icons**
The installation program usually adds an icon to your **Start** menu so that you can easily start the program. If it does not, you can add one for the program. Refer to Task 4, "Adding Programs to the Start Menu."

4 Insert the CD-ROM or floppy disk, and then click the **Next** button.

5 Windows looks on both the floppy disk and the CD-ROM for an installation program. When it finds this file, it displays it in the **Run Installation Program** dialog box.

6 Click the **Finish** button, and then follow the onscreen instructions for your particular program.

End Task

Task 10: Uninstalling Applications

Start Here

You can remove a shortcut icon or an item from the **Start** menu, but doing so leaves that program on your hard disk. When you want to get rid of the program and its files entirely, you can uninstall it. This removes the program and all its related files and folders from your hard disk. You should move any data files from your program folders if, for example, you plan to use them in another program.

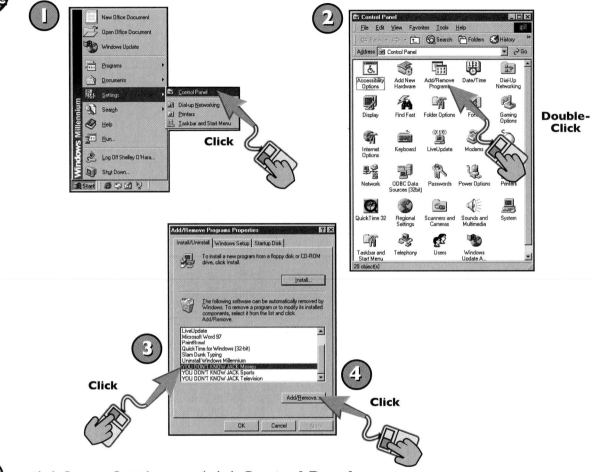

Double-Click

Click

Click

Click

⚠ **WARNING!**
The steps for uninstalling the program will vary from program to program. Simply follow the onscreen instructions.

① Click **Start**, **Settings**, and click **Control Panel**.

② Double-click the **Add/Remove Programs** icon.

③ Click the program you want to remove.

④ Click the **Add/Remove** button.

Next Step

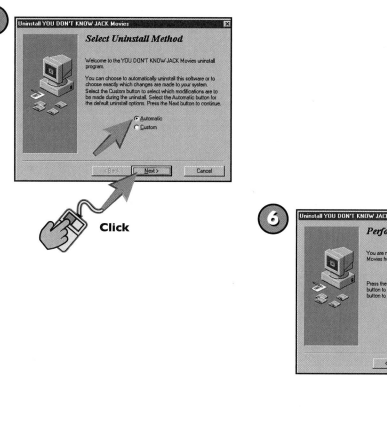

Click

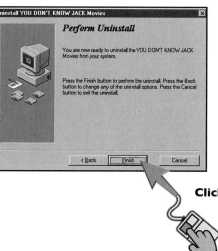

Click

 Program Not Listed?
Some programs can't be uninstalled via the **Install/Uninstall** tab. If your program is not listed, you must use a different procedure. Check your program documentation for specific instructions.

 Uninstall Programs
You can purchase programs to keep track of what programs you have installed, where they are, and what changes they have made to your system. You can use such a program to uninstall programs not listed in the Windows Install/Uninstall tab.

⑤ Follow the onscreen instructions. Some programs, like this one, have an uninstall program. Select how you want to do the uninstall, and click **Next**.

⑥ Click the **Finish** button. The program is removed.

Task 11: Installing Windows Components

If you have a new PC, it probably came with Windows already installed. As a result, you might not know which components are installed and which are not. Likewise, if you have upgraded to Windows Millennium, you might not have installed all the components when you performed the installation. If you want to add components or simply view what else might be available, you can do so.

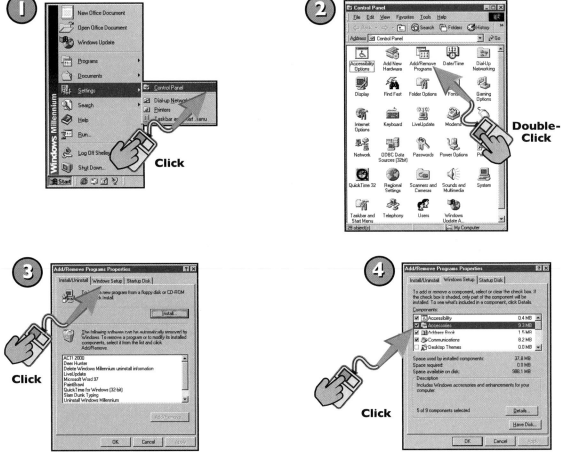

Click

Double-Click

Click

Click

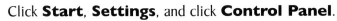

(1) Click **Start**, **Settings**, and click **Control Panel**.

(2) Double-click the **Add/Remove Programs** icon.

(3) Click the **Windows Setup** tab.

(4) Click the feature you want to change or check.

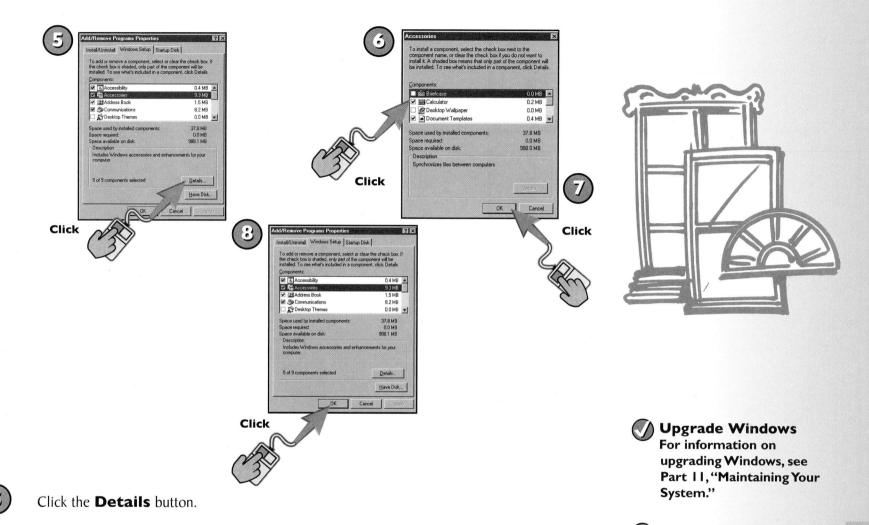

Click (5)

Click (6)

Click (7)

Click (8)

5) Click the **Details** button.

6) You see a list of the available programs for this feature. Check the ones that you want to install, and uncheck any you want to uninstall.

7) Click the **OK** button.

8) Insert your Windows CD-ROM and click **OK** in the **Windows Setup** tab. Files are copied to your system, and the component is available for use.

☑ **Upgrade Windows**
For information on upgrading Windows, see Part 11, "Maintaining Your System."

☑ **Gray Versus Checked**
If an item is checked, it is installed. Items that are gray and checked have some, but not all, of the items installed.

 End Task

Task 12: Using the MS-DOS Prompt

Sometimes you'll want to access the DOS prompt from Windows. For example, you might want to run a DOS application or use DOS commands. (DOS dates back to computers before Windows and is really applicable only for old programs.) Alternatively, you might have programs (especially games) that run in DOS. You can run any program by typing the appropriate DOS command. Windows provides a DOS prompt window that you can open while working in Windows.

Start Here

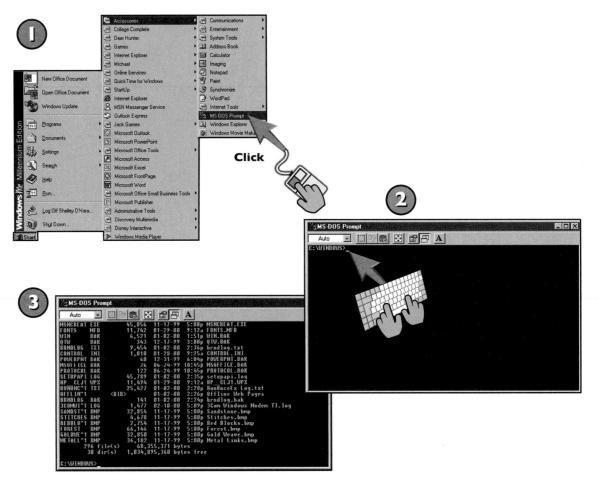

Click

Enlarge the Window
Press **Alt+Enter** to enlarge the DOS window to full screen. Press **Alt+Enter** again to restore the DOS window to its original size.

Close the DOS Prompt
When you are finished working in DOS mode, type **exit** and press **Enter** to close the **MS-DOS Prompt** window.

① Click **Start**, **Programs**, **Accessories**, and click **MS-DOS Prompt**.

② Type the desired command and press **Enter**.

③ You see the results of the command you typed.

End Task

Task 13: Using Run to Start a Program

Start Here

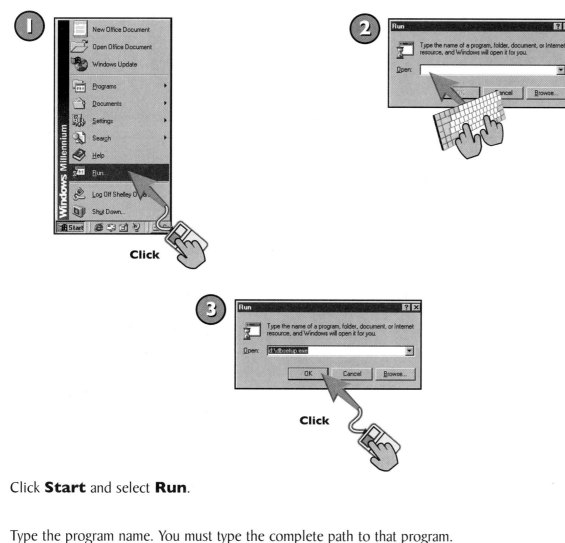

Click

Click

For some programs, especially installation programs, you might need to type the command to run the program. You can also do this for programs you do not use frequently and don't want to set up shortcuts to. To run a program, use the **Run** command. You must know the path and filename of the program you want to open.

Click **Start** and select **Run**.

Type the program name. You must type the complete path to that program.

Click **OK**. The program is started.

Browse
If you don't know the name of the program or its path (drive and folder where it is placed), click the **Browse** button and use the **Browse** dialog box to find the file.

End Task

PART II

Maintaining Your System

This part of the book introduces some techniques that are useful for maintaining your system: defragmenting a disk, backing up data files, scanning a disk for damage, and others. Although you don't have to do these tasks every day, you should periodically do some system housecleaning. For example, you should safeguard your data by making backups or extra copies. If your performance has been slow, you might defragment your disk. Check this section for these and other system enhancements and maintenance.

Tasks

Task 1: Displaying Disk Information

You can display information about your disks, such as the size, the amount of occupied space, and the amount of free space. You can also enter a label for a disk; this label is used in file windows to identify the disk.

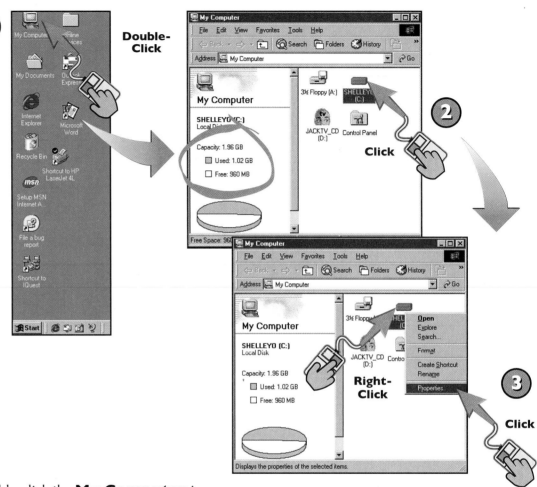

Double-click the **My Computer** icon.

Start Here

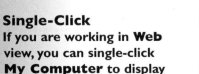

Single-Click
If you are working in **Web** view, you can single-click **My Computer** to display its contents.

In the **My Computer** window, click the disk for which you want information. You see some disk information in the pane on the left of the window.

To get additional information, right-click the disk and select **Properties**.

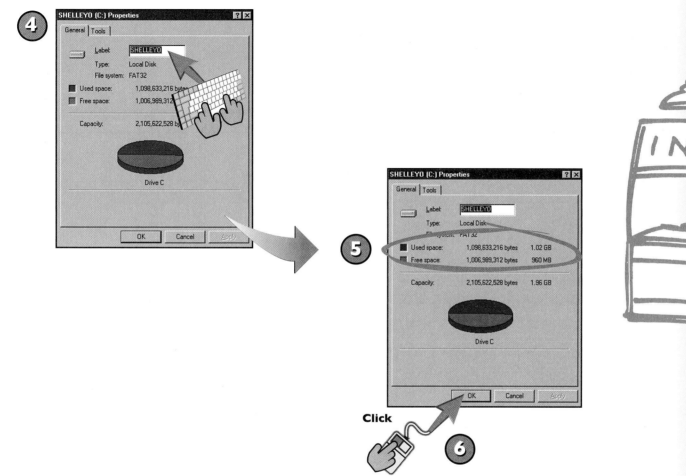

Click

4. If you want, enter a disk label in the **Label** field.

5. View information about used and free space.

6. Click the **OK** button to close the dialog box.

✓ **Use the Tools Tab**
Use the **Tools** tab to select different programs for maintaining your system. This part covers most of the tools found under this tab.

Task 2: Displaying System Information

When you are trouble-shooting, you sometimes need to display information about your system. You can find this information in the **Properties** dialog box for My Computer.

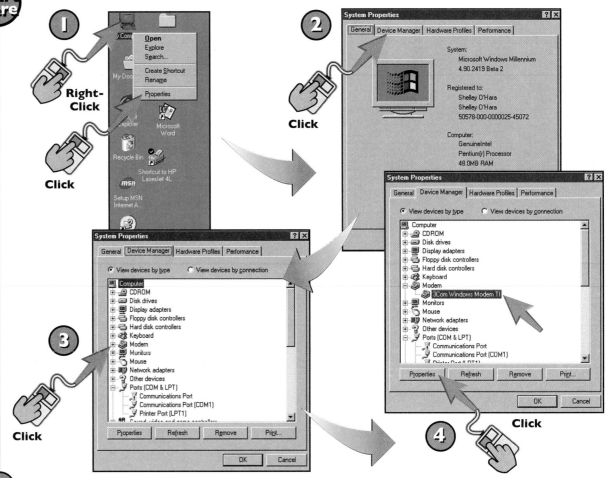

Right-click the **My Computer** icon and choose **Properties**.

You see the **General** tab listing information about the type of computer and the version of Windows. Click the **Device Manager** tab.

You see a list of the devices on your PC. To get detailed information about a device, click the plus sign next to the device type to expand the list.

Select the device and click **Properties**.

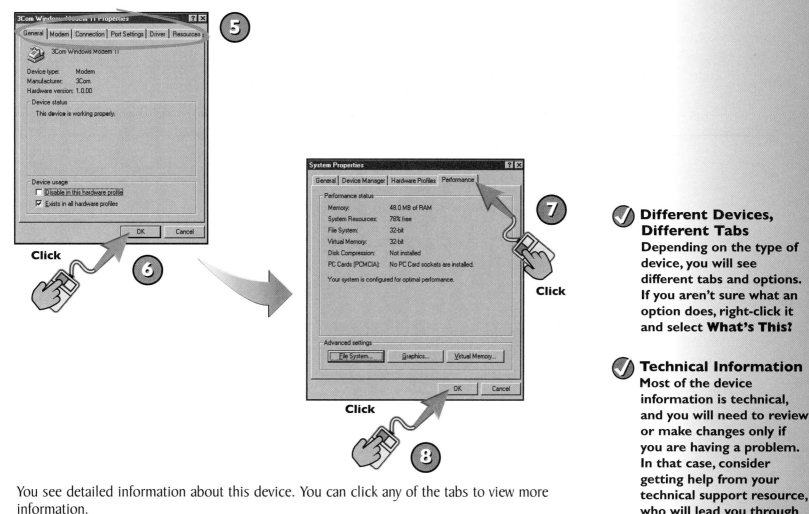

Click

Click

Click

(5) You see detailed information about this device. You can click any of the tabs to view more information.

(6) Click **OK** to close the properties dialog box for the device.

(7) Click the **Performance** tab to view performance information such as the amount of memory.

(8) Click **OK**.

✓ Different Devices, Different Tabs
Depending on the type of device, you will see different tabs and options. If you aren't sure what an option does, right-click it and select **What's This?**

✓ Technical Information
Most of the device information is technical, and you will need to review or make changes only if you are having a problem. In that case, consider getting help from your technical support resource, who will lead you through the steps to make a change based on the hardware experiencing problems. It's usually not a good idea to experiment, especially with advanced settings.

End Task

Task 3: Scanning Your Disk for Errors

Sometimes parts of your hard disk get damaged, and you might see an error message when you try to open or save a file, or you might notice lost or disarrayed data in some of your files. You can scan the disk for damage using the ScanDisk program and fix any problems. You must also run ScanDisk before you can defragment a hard disk (covered next).

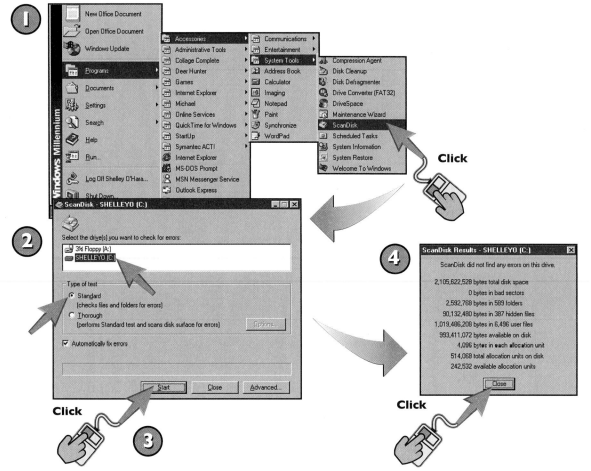

Start Here

Click

Click

Click

Click

✓ Errors Found?

If ScanDisk finds an error, a dialog box appears explaining the error. Read the error message and choose the option that best suits your needs. Click **OK** to continue. Do this for each message.

✓ Scanning After Rebooting

If you don't properly shut down Windows, you are prompted to run ScanDisk when you reboot. You can then check for errors before your system is restarted.

(1) Click **Start**, **Programs**, **Accessories**, **System Tools**, and choose **ScanDisk**.

(2) In the **ScanDisk** dialog box, select the drive you want to scan. In the **Type of test** section, click the radio button next to the type of test you want (**Standard** or **Thorough**).

(3) Click **Start**.

(4) When ScanDisk finishes, it displays a report of the scan. Click **Close** to return to the **ScanDisk** dialog box. Then click **Close** to close the **ScanDisk** dialog box.

Task 4: Cleaning Up Unnecessary Files

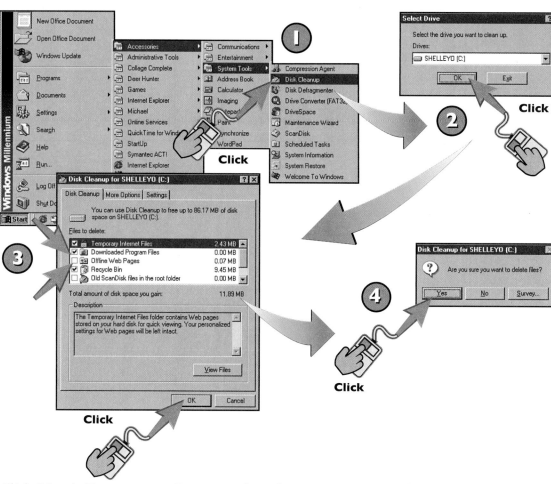

Click

Click

Click

Click

On your system, unnecessary files might be hogging your disk space. Programs such as Internet Explorer store temporary files on your system that you can delete. The Recycle Bin also houses files that you have deleted but are still kept in case you need them. You can easily get rid of these files and gain some disk space.

✓ Review Files
You can view the files that are recommended for removal. Select the files you want to view, and then click the **View Files** button.

✓ WARNING!
Be sure you don't need any of these files. You cannot get them back after they are removed.

1. Click **Start**, **Programs**, **Accessories**, **System Tools**, and choose **Disk Cleanup**.

2. Select the drive you want to clean up, and click **OK**.

3. Windows displays a list of files recommended for removal. Check files you want removed, uncheck files you want to keep, and then click **OK**.

4. When prompted to confirm the removal, click the **Yes** button.

Task 5: Defragmenting a Disk

When a file is stored on your hard drive, Windows places as much of the file as possible in the first available section (called a *cluster*) and then goes to the next cluster to put the next part of the file. Initially, this storage does not cause performance problems, but over time, your disk files become fragmented; you might find that it takes a long time to open a file or start a program. To speed access to files and to help prevent potential problems with fragmented files, you can defragment your disk, putting files in clusters as close to each other as possible. Defragmenting your disk is a general-maintenance job that you should perform every few months for best results.

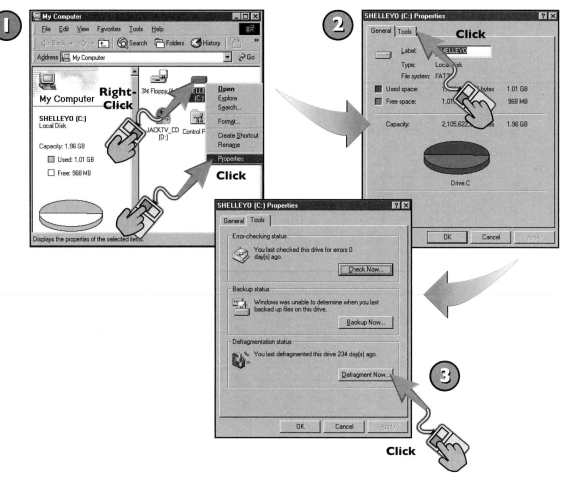

(1) In the **My Computer** window, right-click the disk you want to defragment and select **Properties**.

(2) Click the **Tools** tab.

(3) Click the **Defragment Now** button.

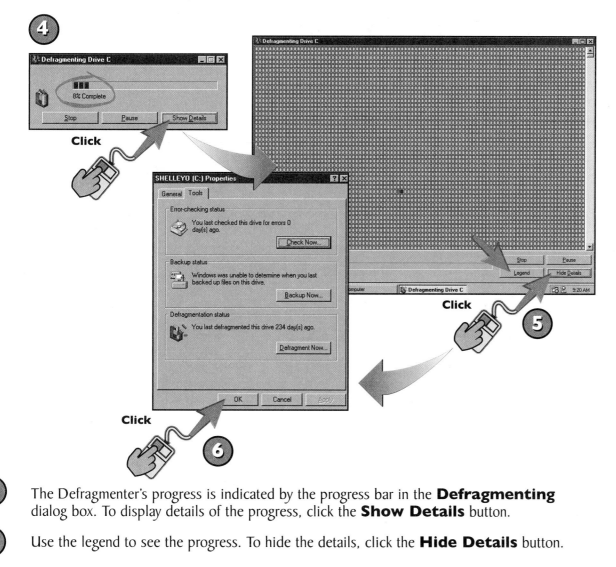

4 The Defragmenter's progress is indicated by the progress bar in the **Defragmenting** dialog box. To display details of the progress, click the **Show Details** button.

5 Use the legend to see the progress. To hide the details, click the **Hide Details** button.

6 When the test is complete, click **Yes** to quit and click the **OK** button to close out the hard disk properties window.

 Defragment Not Necessary
If the disk does not need to be defragmented, Windows displays a message stating that. You can exit or you can defragment anyway.

 Back Up First
Be careful when defragmenting. You might want to back up your data first. See the next task for information about backing up.

End Task

Task 6: Scheduling Tasks

If you perform the same tasks repeatedly, or if you often forget to perform routine maintenance tasks, you can set up a schedule that instructs Windows to perform these tasks automatically.

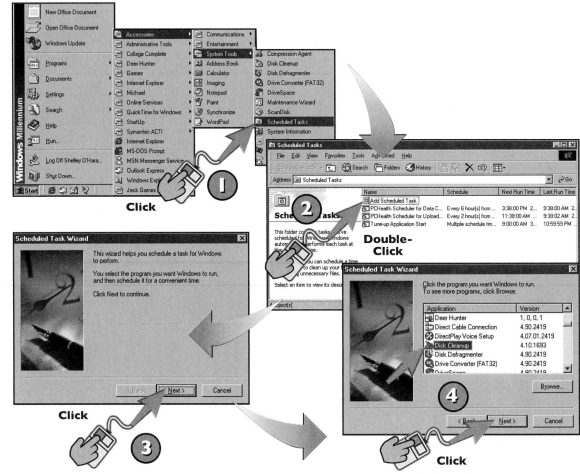

Click

Double-Click

Click

Click

① Click **Start**, **Programs**, **Accessories**, **System Tools**, and then choose **Scheduled Tasks**.

② Double-click the **Add Scheduled Task** list item.

③ Click the **Next** button.

④ Select the name of the program that you want Windows to run, and then click the **Next** button.

Shortcut
You can also double-click the **Scheduled Tasks** icon located in the taskbar to display the **Scheduled Tasks** list.

Next Step

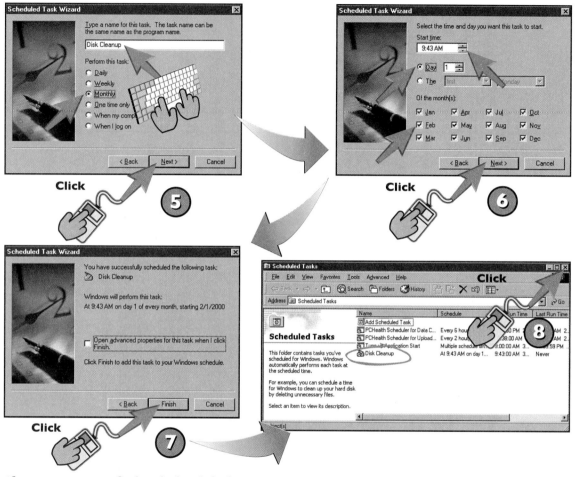

Remove a Task
To remove a task from the list, display the **Scheduled Tasks** list. Right-click the item, and then choose **Delete**. Confirm the deletion by clicking the **Yes** button.

Change Settings
To change the settings for the task (the time, interval, name, and so on), display the **Scheduled Tasks** list. Right-click the item you want to modify, and then choose **Properties**. Make any changes to the tabs in the **Properties** dialog box, and then click **OK**.

No Tasks Listed?
If you have already set up tasks, they are listed in the **Scheduled Tasks** window. If you have not, you can add one.

5 If you are not satisfied with the default name, enter a new one; then select how often to perform this task. Click **Next**.

6 Select the time and date to start. (Depending on how often you select to perform this task, you will see different options for selecting the date and time.) Click **Next**.

7 You see a summary of the scheduled task. Click the **Finish** button.

8 The task is added. Click the **Close** button to close the **Scheduled Tasks** window.

Task 7: Formatting a Floppy Disk

To be able to use a floppy disk, the disk must be formatted. Many disks sold are already formatted, but if they are not or if you want to reformat a disk, you can do so. Keep in mind that formatting a disk erases all the information on that disk.

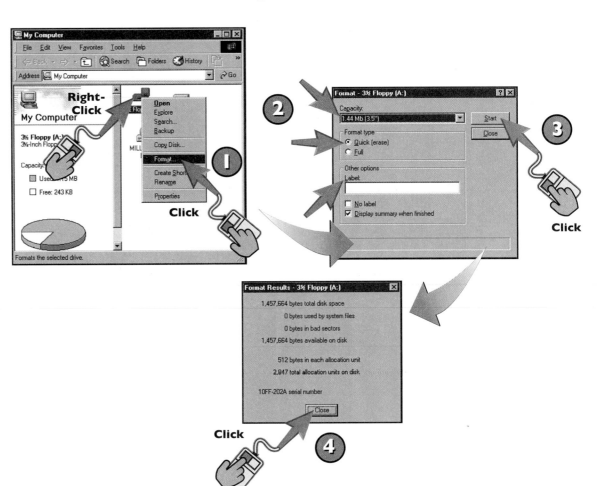

⚠ **WARNING!**
You want to format a hard disk only in the most extreme circumstances. Remember that formatting a disk erases all information on that disk. If you format your hard disk, everything on it will be wiped out, including Windows!

✓ **Create a Startup Disk**
For information on creating a startup disk to use to start your system, see the next task.

① After you've inserted a floppy disk into the drive, open the **My Computer** window. Right-click the floppy disk drive, and choose **Format**.

② Make any changes in the **Capacity** and **Format type** sections (and type a label for the disk if you want).

③ Click **Start**.

④ Windows formats the disk and, when finished, displays a message with details about the disk. To exit, click the **Close** button twice.

Task 8: Creating a Startup Disk

Start Here

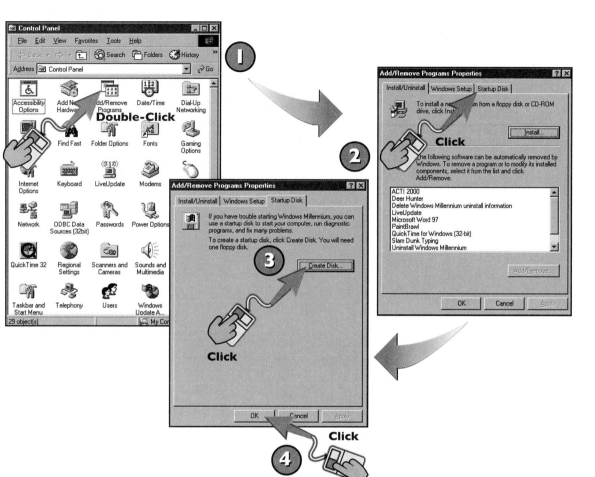

Double-Click

Click

Click

Click

When you start up your system, it first looks for the appropriate startup files on the floppy drive and then goes to the hard drive if it doesn't find them. This startup method ensures that if something is wrong with the hard drive, you can always start from a floppy disk. You can make a startup disk with the necessary files to boot your computer in case of emergency.

1. In the **Control Panel** group, double-click the **Add/Remove Programs** icon.

2. Click the **Startup Disk** tab.

3. Click the **Create Disk** button. Insert a disk when prompted and click **OK**. Windows formats the disk.

4. Click **OK** to close the **Add/Remove Programs Properties** dialog box.

✔ **Open the Control Panel**
To open the Control Panel, click **Start**, select **Settings**, and then select **Control Panel**.

End Task

Task 9: Running the Maintenance Wizard

Included with Windows Millennium is the Maintenance Wizard. You can use this program to handle maintenance tasks such as deleting unnecessary files, checking your hard disk, and speeding up frequently used programs. Simply start the wizard and follow the onscreen prompts.

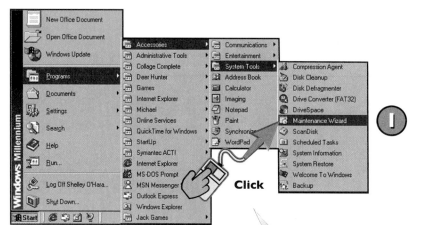

Click

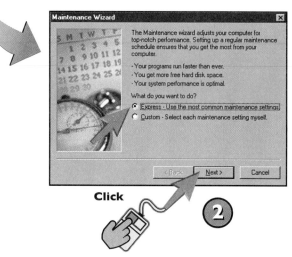

Click

 Click **Start**, **Programs**, **Accessories**, **System Tools**, and then choose **Maintenance Wizard**.

2 Select the **Express** radio button and click **Next**.

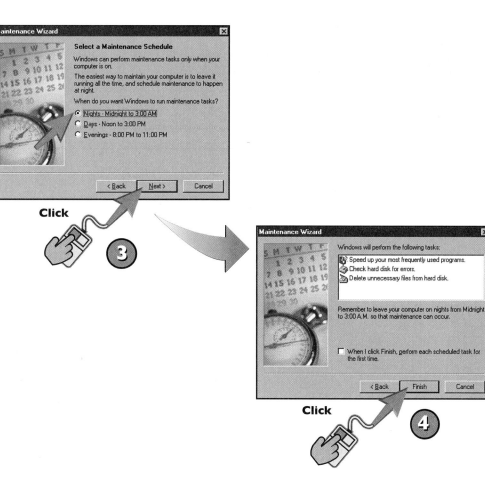

 Select a time to run the maintenance tasks and click **Next**.

 You see a summary of the tasks Windows will perform. Click the **Finish** button.

Click

Click

✓ **Perform Maintenance Now**
If you want to run these tests for the first time immediately, check this option and then click **Finish.** Windows performs the maintenance on your computer, and you see the progress of each test as it is performed.

Task 10: Restoring Your System

If you add new programs or hardware, you might find that your system does not work properly. Trying to troubleshoot a problem such as this can be difficult. To help, Windows includes a new System Restore, which you can use to go back to a previous setup that did work.

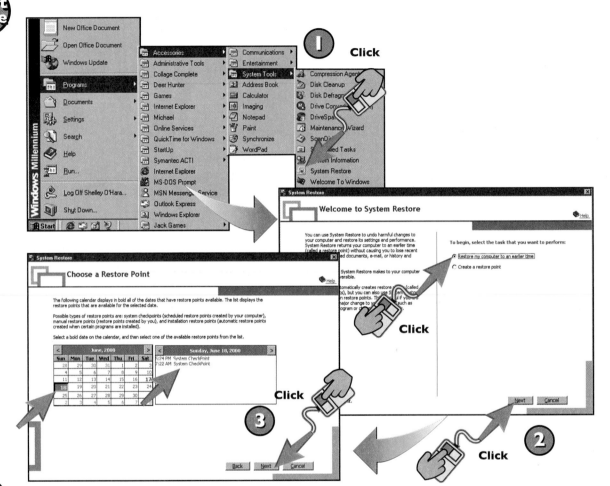

Start Here

Cancel Restore
You can cancel the restore by clicking **Cancel** in any of the dialog boxes. Also, you can go back a step and make a change by clicking **Back**.

① Click **Start**, **Programs**, **Accessories**, **System Tools**, and then choose **System Restore**.

② Select **Restore my Computer to an earlier time**, and then click **Next**.

③ Select a date and time that you want to return to. Then click **Next**.

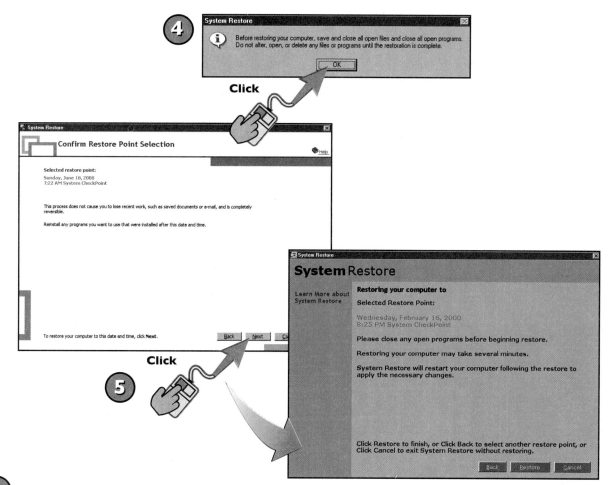

Click

Click

**Create a Restore
Point**
To create a restore point,
click that option and follow
the steps.

Learn More
To get more detailed
information about check-
points and how System
Restore works, click the
Help link in the **System
Restore** dialog box.

4 You see a message about the process. Click **OK**.

5 You see a confirmation of the restore point as well as a list of changes that will be
undone. Click **Next**. Windows restores and restarts your system.

Task II: Installing New Hardware

You can install a new printer, modem, or other hardware device quickly and easily by using Windows's Add New Hardware Wizard. Windows guides you through questions about the hardware, and if you do not know the answers, Windows can detect the type of hardware and install it with little input from you. Windows calls this handy feature *Plug and Play*. This task shows you how to install hardware.

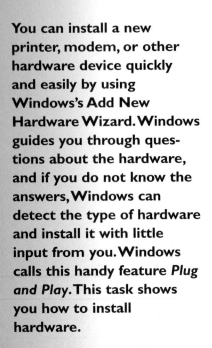

✅ **Connecting the Device**
Connect the new hardware device to your computer by following the instructions that came with the hardware device.

✅ **Steps Vary**
Depending on the type of device, the steps you follow will vary. Simply follow the wizard's instructions, clicking **Next** to go to the next step.

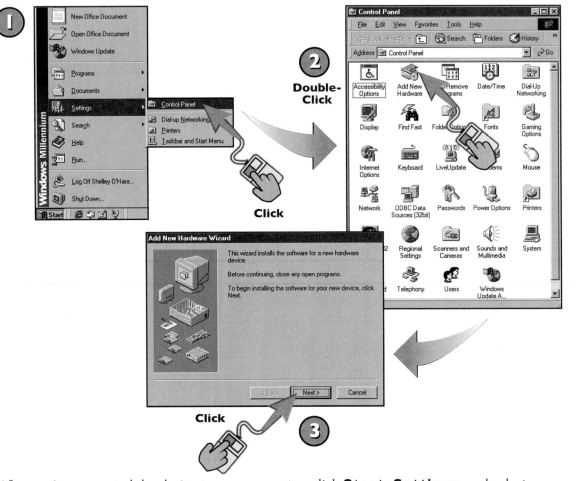

Double-Click

Click

Click

① After you've connected the device to your computer, click **Start**, **Settings**, and select **Control Panel**.

② Double-click the **Add New Hardware** icon.

③ You see an introduction to this wizard. Click the **Next** button.

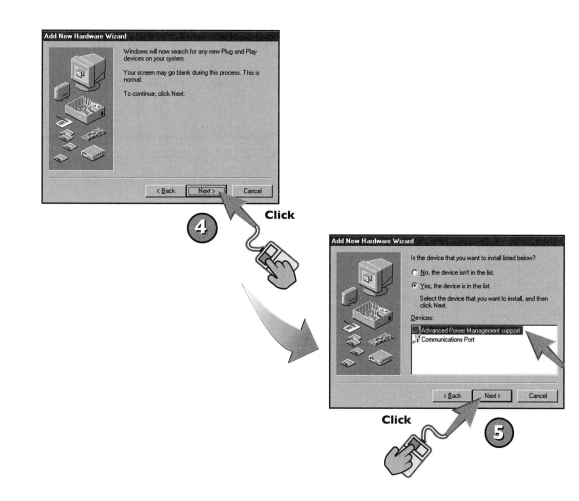

Click

Click

You see a message about searching for Plug and Play devices. Click the **Next** button.

Windows searches your system and displays newly installed hardware. Select the device to install from the **Devices** list, and then click **Next**. Follow the onscreen prompts.

Hardware Not Detected

If the hardware is not automatically detected, you can install it manually. Select **No, the device isn't in the list**. Click **Next** and follow the onscreen instructions.

Automatic Setup

If Windows detected your hardware, it is set up automatically. You might be prompted to insert the appropriate software disks to set up the hardware. Follow the onscreen directions.

End Task

Home Networking Basics

The term *network* can refer generically to any situation in which two or more computers are linked to share information. The Internet qualifies as a network, as do local area networks (LANs), wide area networks (WANs), and so on. But in this part, I will be focusing on home networks consisting of just a few PCs.

To network your home computers, each computer will need a network interface card (NIC). If you have more than two PCs to network, you will also need a *hub*, which is a separate box into which cables from each network card connect. Many home networking kits you can buy contain the cards and the hub, as well as setup instructions.

With the networking hardware installed, you must set up each PC to use the network. Windows Millennium comes with a **Home Networking Wizard** that configures a PC for networking, so it is not the difficult and intimidating task that you might think.

Tasks

Task 1: Configuring a PC for Networking

After you have installed the networking hardware, you can configure each computer to use the network by working through the **Home Networking Wizard.** This wizard automates several procedures that were once done manually in earlier versions of Windows, including configuring for file and printer sharing. It also sets up Internet Connection Sharing (ICS) automatically, so multiple PCs can share a single Internet connection.

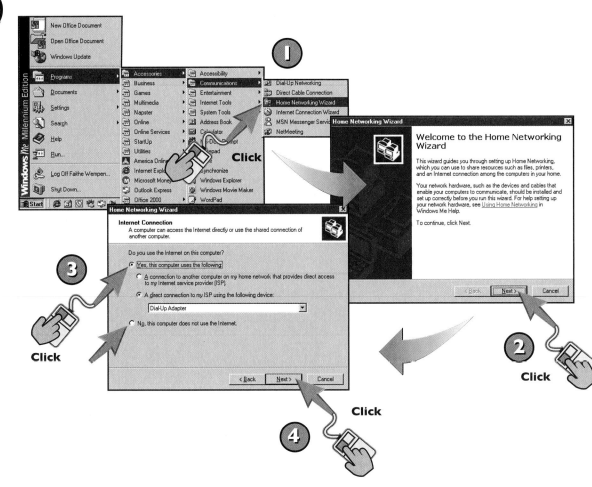

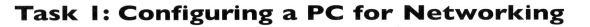

Internet Connection
If you do not yet have an Internet connection to your ISP set up on this PC, you might want to do that before setting up a home network. See Part 7, "Connecting to Online Services and the Internet."

1 Choose **Start, Programs, Accessories, Communications, Home Networking Wizard.**

2 When the **Home Networking Wizard** window appears, click **Next** to begin setting up your home network.

3 Choose **Yes** or **No** to indicate whether this PC uses the Internet or connects to the Internet through a different PC on your network.

4 If you chose **Yes** in step 3, choose how that connection is made, and then click **Next** to continue.

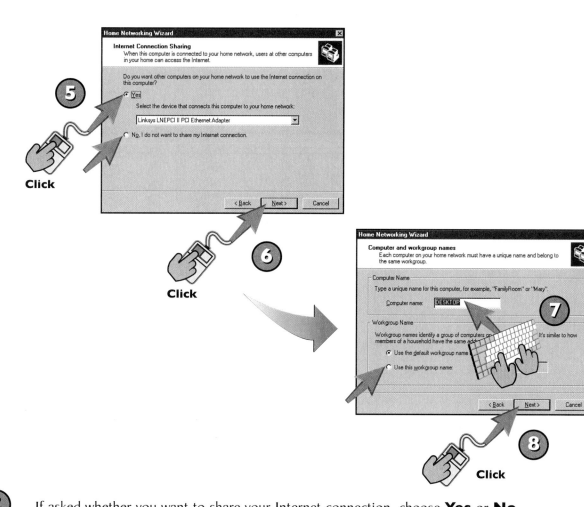

Connection Sharing
With Windows Millennium (and Windows 98 SE as well), all the PCs on your network can share the Internet connection of a single PC. Each networked PC can surf the Web and work with email simultaneously, provided the PC with the actual Internet connection is turned on and online.

Is NIC Installed?
If your network interface card does not appear on the list in step 6, you will want to cancel the home networking setup for now and ensure that your NIC is installed properly.

Computer Name
This will give your computer a name that both you and the network can use to identify this PC.

Workgroup Name
All the computers on your home network must use the same workgroup name, so it is best to accept the default name unless you already have a home network set up with a different workgroup name and you are merely adding a new computer to it.

(5) If asked whether you want to share your Internet connection, choose **Yes** or **No**.

(6) If you chose **Yes** in step 5, select your NIC from the list if it does not appear already, and click **Next** to continue.

(7) Enter a name for this computer in the **Computer name** box.

(8) Accept the default workgroup name of MSHOME (or select **Use this workgroup name** to choose your own), and click **Next** to continue.

Task 1: Configuring a PC for Networking Continued

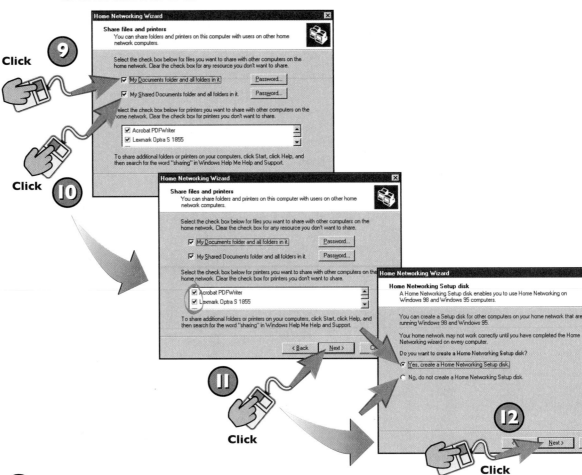

Click ⑨

Click ⑩

Click ⑪

⑫

Click

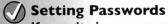

Setting Passwords

If security is a concern on your home network, you can add password protection to your **My Documents** and **My Shared Documents** folders by clicking the appropriate **Password** button and typing a password. If you do not set any passwords, a warning will appear after you click **Next**. Click **OK** to acknowledge it, and then click **Next** to continue.

Printers

Some devices on the list of printers might not actually be printers; you might find fax drivers, PDFWriter drivers, and so on there.

⑨ To share the contents of **My Documents** with the other computers on the network, mark the **My Documents folder and all folders in it** check box.

⑩ To share the contents of **My Shared Documents**, mark the **My Shared Documents folder and all folders in it** check box.

⑪ To decline to share a printer with other computers on the network, deselect its check box and click **Next** to continue.

⑫ If you have Windows 95/98 computers to set up for the home network, choose **Yes**. Otherwise choose **No** and click **Next** to continue.

Next Step

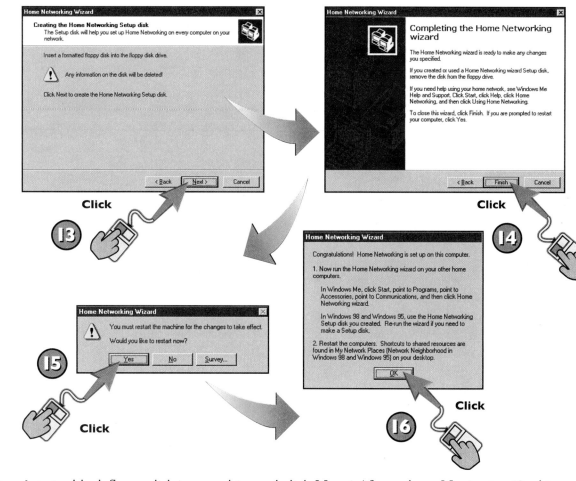

Setup Disk
The setup disk contains a program called Setup.exe. Run this program on a Windows 95/98 PC to set it up to work with your home network. To run the setup program, insert the setup disk in the Windows 95/98 PC's floppy drive. Double-click **My Computer**, double-click the **A:** drive icon, and then double-click the **Setup.exe** file icon.

Restarting Is Necessary
Make sure you restart your computer when prompted, because Windows has modified some important system files. If you continue operating Windows without restarting, you could experience problems.

Other PCs
Repeat this procedure on each Windows Millennium PC to set up on the network. If you need to set up a Windows 95/98 PC, insert the setup disk you created in that PC and run the Setup.exe program on that disk.

13 Insert a blank floppy disk in your drive and click **Next** (if you chose **No** in step 12, skip ahead to the next step).

14 Click **Finish**.

15 Click **Yes** to restart.

16 After Windows reboots, a message will pop up confirming successful setup of your home network. Click **OK**.

Task 2: Accessing Network Files

You can browse shared files on the network through the **My Network Places** icon on your desktop. It works just like **My Computer**, except that it shows you files on other network computers instead of the ones on your system.

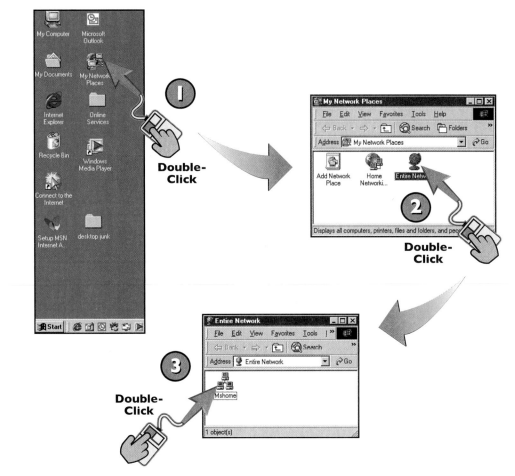

Which Workgroup?
You will probably have only one workgroup in step 3. If you have more than one, choose the one connecting the computers you want to access.

① Double-click **My Network Places** icon on the desktop.

② Double-click **Entire Network**.

③ Double-click the name of your workgroup.

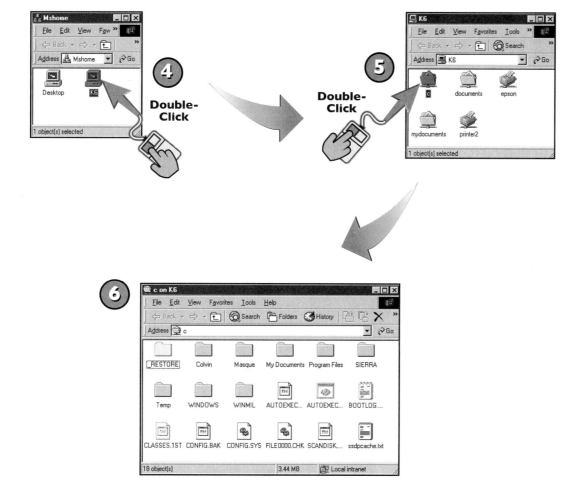

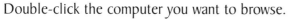

④ Double-click the computer you want to browse.

⑤ Double-click the drive or folder you want to browse.

⑥ Work with the files and folders normally, as you would files on your local hard disk.

✅ **Computer Contents**
The window that appears when you double-click the computer shows icons for each shared drive plus any individually shared folders. It also has icons for the shared printers, so you can display and manage the printers' queues.

✅ **File Management Help**
Refer to Part 2, "Working with Disks, Folders, and Files," if you need help working with files and folders.

Task 3: Mapping a Network Drive

Not all programs enable you to browse network locations when opening or saving files. Some programs can only recognize drives on your computer. For the benefit of such programs, you can trick Windows into thinking that a particular drive or folder on the network is actually located on your system. This is called *mapping a network drive*. To do this, you create a connection that leads all programs from an imaginary new drive letter on your system to the network location you want. For example, you could assign the drive letter J: to a folder on the network called D:\Arts, so that whenever you display the contents of your J: drive, you are actually displaying the contents of that folder. After mapping a drive, the new letter appears in all drive listings.

(I) After using **My Network Places** to view a network computer, display and select the network drive that you want to map.

(2) Right-click the drive icon and click **Map Network Drive**.

(3) Open the **Drive** drop-down list and click the drive letter you want to use for the drive.

(4) Mark the **Reconnect at logon** check box if you want this mapping to be active every time you log on, and click **OK**.

Task 4: Creating Network Shortcuts

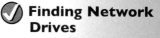

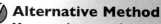

Right- Click Drag

Drop

Click

You don't have to browse the entire network each time you want to use a particular network drive or folder; you can simply create a shortcut to it and use that shortcut.

Finding Network Drives
Refer to Task 2, "Accessing Network Files," to learn about accessing a network disk drive.

Alternative Method
You can, in many instances, type the location of the network drive or folder into the address window in Windows Explorer or your Web browser. Typically, you will begin the network share or folder with two backward slashes ****, like this: **\\computer\ drivename**.

1 Display the drive or folder's icon in **My Network Places**, as you learned earlier in this part.

2 Right-click and drag the icon onto the desktop. When you release the mouse button, a shortcut menu appears.

3 Choose **Create Shortcut(s) Here** from the menu that appears and Windows will place the shortcut on your desktop.

In addition to creating a network shortcut on your desktop, you can also create one that appears in the **My Network Places** window. This shortcut can point to any computer, drive, or folder on the network.

Task 5: Creating Network Shortcuts in My Network Places

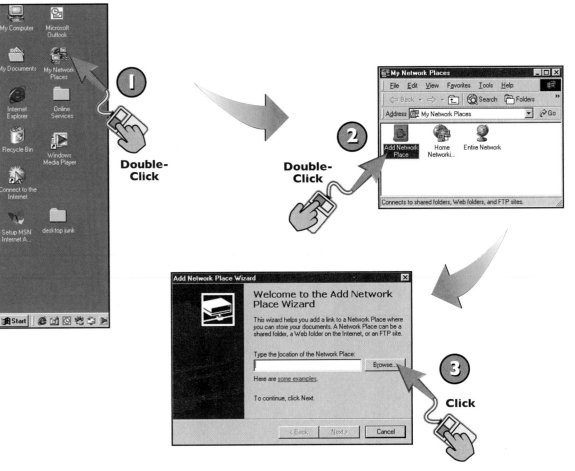

Enter Network Path
If you know the network path, you can type it in the **Network Place** box instead of doing steps 3 through 5. Make sure you start out with \\ to indicate a network path.

1. Double-click **My Network Places** on the desktop.

2. Double-click **Add Network Place**. The **Add Network Place Wizard** opens.

3. Click the **Browse** button. A **Browse for Folder** dialog box appears.

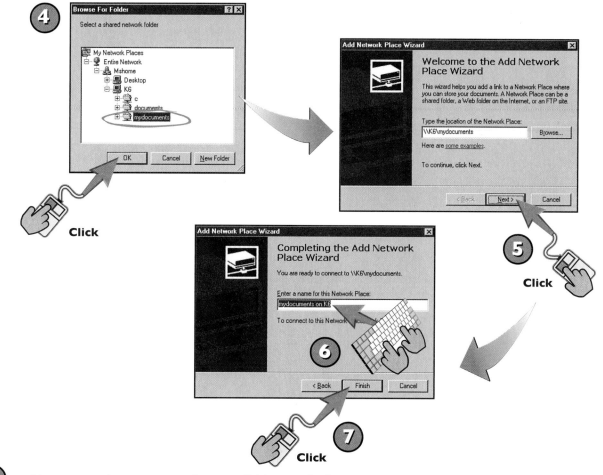

Browse For Folder
Select a shared network folder

- My Network Places
  - Entire Network
    - Mshome
      - Desktop
      - K6
        - c
        - documents
        - *mydocuments*

OK   Cancel   New Folder

Click

Add Network Place Wizard

Welcome to the Add Network Place Wizard

This wizard helps you add a link to a Network Place where you can store your documents. A Network Place can be a shared folder, a Web folder on the Internet, or an FTP site.

Type the location of the Network Place:

\\K6\mydocuments   Browse...

Here are some examples.

To continue, click Next.

< Back   Next >   Cancel

⑤ **Click**

Add Network Place Wizard

Completing the Add Network Place Wizard

You are ready to connect to \\K6\mydocuments.

Enter a name for this Network Place:

mydocuments on K6

To connect to this Network...

⑥

< Back   Finish   Cancel

⑦ **Click**

④ Navigate to the computer, drive, or folder to which you want to create a shortcut. Select it and click **OK**.

⑤ Click **Next** to continue.

⑥ Type a name for the shortcut.

⑦ Click **Finish**.

✓ **Shortcut Name**
The shortcut name can be a "friendly" or descriptive name; it need not match the actual drive or folder name.

✓ **Shortcut Created**
The chosen computer, drive, or folder appears in an Explorer window. From then on, the shortcut to that place appears in your **My Network Places** window.

Task 6: Printing to a Network Printer

A network printer works the same as a local printer in all your applications. Simply select the printer from the **Print** dialog box in whatever program you are printing from.

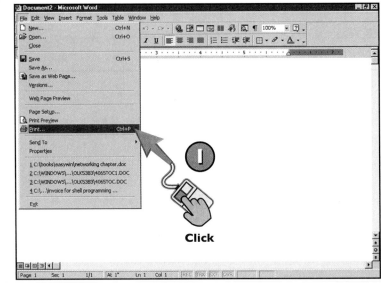

Click

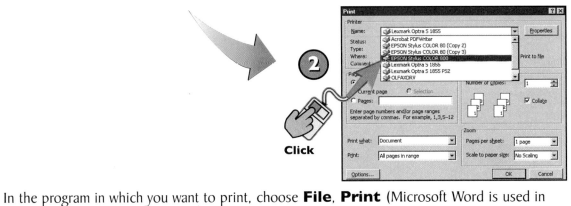

Click

 In the program in which you want to print, choose **File**, **Print** (Microsoft Word is used in this example).

 Open the **Name** drop-down list and choose the network printer.

✓ Windows Consistency
Microsoft Word is shown as an example here, but the process works the same in all Windows-based programs.

Next Step

③ Click **OK**, and Windows prints the document across the network to the selected printer.

Click

✅ **Network Printers**
The network printers can be distinguished from the local printers by a slightly different icon with a horizontal bar beneath it (see step 2).

A

accessory   One of the miniapplications that comes free with Windows Millennium. Examples include WordPad, Paint, and Backup.

Active Desktop   A feature you can turn on to display Web content on your desktop.

active window   The window you're currently using. You can tell a window is active by looking at its title bar: If the bar shows white letters on a dark background, the window is active. Inactive windows show light gray letters on a dark gray background.

application   Software that accomplishes a specific practical task. Same thing as a program.

application window   A window that contains a running application, such as Paint or WordPad.

ASCII text file   A file that uses only the American Standard Code for Information Interchange character set (techno-lingo for the characters you see on your keyboard).

B

backup job   A list of files to back up, the type of backup to use (full, differential, or incremental), and the backup destination.

boot   To start your computer. The term booting comes from the phrase "pulling oneself up by one's own bootstraps," which refers to the fact that your computer can load everything it needs to operate properly without any help from you.

bps   Bits per second. The rate at which a modem or other communications device sends data through a phone line or cable.

browser   A program that you use to view sites on the World Wide Web. The browser that comes with Windows Millennium is called Internet Explorer.

byte   A single character of information.

C

cascade menu   A menu that appears when you select certain pull-down menu commands.

CD-ROM drive   A special computer disk drive that's designed to handle CD-ROM discs, which resemble audio CDs. CD-ROMs have enormous capacity (about 500 times that of a typical floppy disk), so they're most often used to hold large applications, graphics libraries, and huge collections of shareware programs.

channel   A special World Wide Web site that features changing content.

character formatting   Changing the look of text characters by altering their font, size, style, and more.

character spacing   The amount of space a font reserves for each character. In a monospaced font, every character gets the same amount of space regardless of its true width. In a proportional font, the space allotted to each letter varies according to the width of the letter.

check box   A square-shaped switch that toggles a dialog box option on or off. The option is toggled on when a check mark appears in the box.

classic desktop   The folder view used with Windows 95. Contrast this with Active Desktop.

click   To quickly press and release the left mouse button.

Clipboard An area of memory that holds data temporarily during cut-and-paste operations.

command button A rectangular "button" (usually found in dialog boxes) that, when clicked, runs whatever command is spelled out on it.

commands The options you see in a pull-down menu. You use these commands to tell the application what you want it to do next.

D

data files The files used by you or your programs. See also *program files*.

desktop A metaphor for the screen that you see when Windows Millennium starts. Starting a Windows Millennium application is similar to putting a folder full of papers (the application window) on your desk. To do some work, you pull some papers out of the folder (the document windows) and place them on the desktop.

device driver A small program that controls the way a device (such as a mouse or printer) works with your system.

dialog boxes Windows that pop up on the screen to ask you for information or to seek confirmation of an action you requested.

differential backup Backs up only files in the current backup job that have changed since the last full backup. See also *incremental backup*.

digital camera A special camera that saves pictures using digital storage (such as a memory card) instead of film.

directory See *folder*.

diskette See *floppy disk*.

document window A window opened in an application. Document windows hold whatever you're working on in the application.

double-click To quickly press and release the left mouse button twice in succession.

double-click speed The maximum amount of time Windows Millennium allows between the mouse clicks of a double-click.

drag To press and hold down the left mouse button and then move the mouse.

drag-and-drop A technique you use to run commands or move things around; you use your mouse to drag files or icons to strategic screen areas and drop them there.

drop-down list box A list box that normally shows only a single item but, when selected, displays a list of options.

DVD A type of storage medium similar to a CD-ROM but with better sound, graphics, and video quality. Some computers now come with a DVD drive rather than a CD-ROM drive. You can find movies and programs on DVDs. You can also use standard data and audio CDs in a DVD drive.

E–F

Explorer bar The left pane of a folder window. You can choose to display different lists in this area, including a Folders list, a History list, or a Favorites list.

Favorites A list of folders, files, or Web sites. You can add items to the Favorites list and then quickly access the item.

file An organized unit of information inside your computer.

floppy disk A portable storage medium that consists of a flexible magnetic disk protected by a plastic case. Floppy disks are available in a variety of sizes and capacities.

folder A storage location on your hard disk in which you keep related files together.

Folder list A list of the drives and folders on your system. In folder windows, you can display the Folder list by clicking the Folders button.

font A character set of a specific typeface, type style, and type size.

format bar A series of text boxes and buttons that enable you to format the characters in your document. The format bar typically appears under the toolbar.

formatting The process of setting up a disk so that a drive can read its information and write information to it. Not to be confused with character formatting.

fragmented When a single file is chopped up and stored in separate chunks scattered around a hard disk. You can fix this by running Windows Millennium's Disk Defragmenter program.

full backup Backs up all the files in the current backup job. See also *differential backup* and *incremental backup*.

G–I

Gaming options New features in Windows Millennium that enable you to set options for how games are installed as well as how game controllers are set up.

gigabyte 1,024 megabytes. Those in-the-know usually abbreviate this as GB when writing, and as gig when speaking. See also *byte*, *kilobyte*, and *megabyte*.

hard disk A storage medium that consists of several metallic disks stacked on top of each other, usually protected by a metal outer case. Hard disks are available in a variety of sizes and capacities and are usually the main storage area inside your computer.

History A list of folders, files, or Web sites you have opened recently. You can display the History list and then select to view any of the items in the list.

hover To place the mouse pointer over an object for a few seconds. In most Windows applications, for example, if you hover the mouse over a toolbar

button, a small banner shows up that tells you the name of the button.

icons The little pictures that Windows Millennium uses to represent programs and files.

incremental backup Backs up only files in the current backup job that have changed since the last full backup or the last differential backup.

infrared port A communications port, usually found on notebook computers and some printers. Infrared ports enable two devices to communicate by using infrared light waves instead of cables.

insertion point cursor The blinking vertical bar you see inside a text box or in a word-processing application, such as WordPad. It indicates where the next character you type will appear.

Internet A network of networks that extends around the world. You can access this network by setting up an account with an Internet service provider.

intranet The implementation of Internet technologies for use within a corporate organization rather than for connection to the Internet as a whole.

IR Short for infrared. See *infrared port*.

ISP Stands for Internet service provider. The company that provides access to the Internet. You dial and connect to this network. You have access to the entire Internet through the ISP's network.

J–L

Jaz drive A special disk drive that uses portable disks (about the size of floppy disks) that hold I gigabyte of data.

Kbps One thousand bits per second (bps). Today's modern modems transmit data at either 28.8Kbps or 56Kbps.

keyboard delay The amount of time it takes for a second character to appear when you press and hold down a key.

kilobyte 1,024 bytes. This is often abbreviated K or KB. See also *megabyte* and *gigabyte*.

LAN See *local area network*.

local area network A network in which all the computers occupy a relatively small geographical area, such as a department, an office, a home, or a building. All the connections between computers are made via network cables.

list box A small window that displays a list of items such as filenames or directories.

M

maximize To increase the size of a window to its largest extent. A maximized application window fills the entire screen except for the taskbar. A maximized document window fills the entire application window.

Mbps One million bits per second (bps).

megabyte 1,024 kilobytes, or 1,048,576 bytes. This is often abbreviated in writing to M or MB and pronounced meg. See also *gigabyte*.

memory-resident program A program that stays in memory after it is loaded and works "behind the scenes." The program normally responds only to a specific event (such as the deletion of a file) or key combination. Also called a terminate-and-stay-resident (TSR) program.

menu bar The horizontal bar on the second line of an application window. The menu bar contains the application's pull-down menus.

minimize Removing a program from the desktop without closing it. A button for the program remains on the taskbar.

modem An electronic device that enables two computers to exchange data over phone lines.

multitasking The capability to run several programs at the same time.

N–P

network A collection of computers connected using special cables or other network media (such as infrared ports) to share files, folders, disks, peripherals, and applications. See also *local area network*.

newsgroup An Internet discussion group devoted to a single topic. These discussions progress by "posting" messages to the group.

option buttons See *radio buttons*.

point To place the mouse pointer so that it rests on a specific screen location.

port The connection into which you plug the cable from a device such as a mouse or printer.

program files The files that run your programs. See also *data files*.

pull-down menus   Hidden menus that you open from an application's menu bar to access the commands and features of the application.

radio buttons   Dialog box options that appear as small circles in groups of two or more. Only one option from a group can be chosen. These are also called option buttons.

RAM   Stands for random access memory. The memory in your computer that Windows Millennium uses to run your programs.

repeat rate   After the initial delay, the rate at which characters appear when you press and hold down a key.

right-click   To click the right mouse button instead of the usual left button. In Windows Millennium, right-clicking something usually pops up a shortcut menu.

S

scalable font   A font in which each character exists as an outline that can be scaled to different sizes. Windows Millennium includes such scalable fonts as Arial, Courier New, and Times New Roman. To use scalable fonts, you must have a software program called a type manager to do the scaling. Windows

Millennium comes with its own type manager, TrueType.

scrollbar   A bar that appears at the bottom or on the right side of a window when the window is too small to display all its contents.

shortcut   A special file that points to a program or a document. Double-clicking the shortcut starts the program or loads the document.

shortcut menu   A menu that contains a few commands related to an item (such as the desktop or the taskbar). You display the shortcut menu by right-clicking the object.

surf   To travel from site to site on the World Wide Web.

system resources   Memory areas that Windows Millennium uses to keep track of things such as the position and size of open windows, dialog boxes, and your desktop configuration (wallpaper and so on).

T

taskbar   The horizontal strip across the bottom of the Windows Millennium screen. Each running application is given its own taskbar button, and you switch to an application by clicking its button. Sometimes called the system tray.

text box   A screen area in which you type text information, such as a description or a filename.

text editor   A program that lets you edit files that contain only text. The Windows Millennium text editor is called Notepad.

title bar   The area on the top line of a window that displays the window's title.

toolbar   A series of application-specific buttons that typically appears beneath the menu bar.

tracking speed   The speed at which the mouse pointer moves across the screen when you move the mouse on its pad.

TrueType   A font-management program that comes with Windows Millennium.

type size   A measurement of the height of a font. Type size is measured in points; there are 72 points in an inch.

type style   Character attributes, such as regular, bold, and italic. Other type styles (often called type effects) are underline and strikethrough.

typeface   A distinctive graphic design of letters, numbers, and other symbols.

U–W

Web integration The integration of World Wide Web techniques into the Windows Millennium interface. See *Web view*.

Web view A folder view that enables you to single-click an icon to open it. You can also add Web content to your desktop. See *Active Desktop*.

window A rectangular screen area in which Windows Millennium displays applications and documents.

word wrap A word-processor feature that automatically starts a new line when your typing reaches the end of the current line.

write protection Floppy disk safeguard that prevents you from changing any information on the disk. On a 3 1/2-inch disk, write protection is controlled by a small movable tab on the back of the disk. If the tab is toward the edge of the disk, the disk is write protected. To disable the write protection, slide the tab away from the edge of the disk.

X–Z

Zip drive A special disk drive that uses portable disks (a little smaller than a Jaz drive disk) that hold 100 megabytes of data.

A

displaying

E

RAM (random access memory)

W - Z

WordPad